THIS COPY
SIGNED

IRRATIONAL
HOPE

Moving From Pain To Purpose

D1712920

Robert Ryan

Cover Image – Cover was created by Delos Studio.

Except were specifically credited, other images used in the book were created by the author. Some author created images make use backgrounds purchased from depositphotos.com or sourced from copyright-free and royalty-free sites PixaBay.com, Freepik.com, FreeSVG.com, and Freerangephotos.com. Further details are provided in the Images Section at the end of the book.

Unless otherwise noted, all Scripture quotations are taken from the Holy Bible, New Revised Standard Version Catholic Edition - NRSVCE, with the imprimatur of the United States Conference of Catholic Bishops, (Libreria Editrice Vaticana, Catholic Bible Press, Apr 6, 2014) Available at: https://www.biblegateway.com

Editri Domici

Houston

1st Edition

Copyright © 2023 By Robert G. Ryan

All rights reserved.

ISBN: 979-8-3924-0991-4

If you can't count on tomorrow, make today count.

Contents

Prologue

I wrote this book to better understand my pain and suffering as a recurrent cancer patient, and to live each precious day in a better way. Time weighs most on those who have it least, and I wish to spend my remaining time on living, for my death needs none of it.

We all suffer, but if you struggle with why that's true and with how to find hope to go on, please read this book. I know pain and suffering intimately, and I share my journey from the darkest depths of hysterical sadness to acceptance, understanding, and joy. In this book we explore the purpose of suffering and show you how to gain from it. We do this not on a grand humanity level, but on a vulnerable, personal level, with unique insights that will make a difference in how you live and how you approach death.

My cancer is terminal, yet each day I hope for physical and spiritual healing. If left only to what man can do, this would be *Irrational Hope.* But my hope rests not in man, but in God; for God is not limited by what I can do. When I base my hope on the possibilities of what God can do, the irrational becomes rational.

Most of us must first be humbled by pain, tragedy, and loss to find the truth of it all. What follows are my truths and the insights that have helped me on my journey. I hope they help you too.

While this book is laid out in a logical progression, each chapter largely stands on its own. Therefore, feel free to select the chapter that interests you most, and read outward from there.

My Truths

Before sharing insights regarding the practice and the purpose of pain and suffering as taken from the depths of my own repeated struggle with a rare cancer, it is important to summarize what I have come to know as truths in my physical and spiritual journey.

What I believe to be true to the deepest depths of my mind and soul:

- That there is a God
- That God is the purposeful designer of the universe around us
- That God, the Lawgiver, is not in conflict with science and the natural laws of the universe, for they are both true and part of the same truth
- That God, the essence of being itself, is the source of everything from nothing
- That God is the transcendent being our mortal selves reflect and seek
- That God is perfect, but our natural world is not, for what comes with imperfection is the freedom to love, to turn toward or away from God
- That God is a God who walked both mortal and divine among us, as Jesus
- That God suffered and died as a man so that we have a path through Him and to Him
- That God asks of us only that we freely love Him and our fellow man
- That God is not the source of evil, pain, and suffering in our world, but the source of their defeat
- That God is everlasting and our source of all hope and our everlasting life with him

While I cannot scientifically prove my beliefs above, I am a scientific and evidence-based Christian, and my beliefs are all rooted in reason. It was Francis Bacon (1561–1626) who introduced the use of scientific experimentation and induction as a path to truth. Building on the works of St. Augustine, he argued in his book, *Advancement of Learning*,[1] that God has two books, the book of nature and the book of His word.

I believe both books are true and both books are crucial to understanding the meaning of life and the world around us. I have studied each extensively and have yet to find a material contradiction. I have yet to find a need to choose between them. A book is a representation of reality, not reality itself. If two books by the same perfect author appear to be inconsistent with one another, the problem is with the understanding of the interpreter, not the author.

I have reasoned my way to a belief in a God of intelligent design, and I know as a fact that Jesus was a historical figure. My faith comes into play only in the nature of my relationship with Christ and God the Father. I understand the natural world as well as all the laws of physics so far discovered as to the workings of this universe. I believe these laws as ardently as any atheist. I also know there is something more.

The Depth of Pain

"I am sunk in the abysmal swamp where there is no foothold; I have reached the watery depths; the flood overwhelms me." Psalm 69:14[2]

Hysterical Sadness is a term I use to reference the darkness that surrounded me after my latest recurrent cancer diagnosis, my seventh cancer surgery, chemo, radiation, and immunotherapy. It is a lonely place where only the tiniest sliver of hope remains. A place where you have no control over your pain and suffering, and only the slightest control over what you do with it. A place where weeping has no end yet gives no relief. A place where only sadness remains. Hysterical because it has no useful purpose and seemingly no end. A deep despair rooted in the fear that my faith, my God, has failed me.

How does it end? It ends only in the exhaustion of sadness itself. A moment of complete humility, helplessness, and surrender. At that moment there appears a glimmer of light, a light of hope that goes beyond our mortal existence. A light of hope that comes only through a sense, however weak, of the presence of Christ within us, a sharing of our suffering by a God made man so that He might suffer as man, and so transcend that suffering, and bring us to Himself. A God, who through His own human death on the cross, has shown us that hope remains. Hope manifest in Christ's resurrection, Christ's victory over our human death, Christ's gift of eternal life through Him, through the path that He has provided, and through a door that He has left open.

I do not merit entry, but Christ requires nothing of me other than my love for Him. I have nothing else to give, and the beauty is that my love is sufficient. My love is beautifully the only currency I have and the only currency God accepts. He first gave me the very love I return to Him.

My salvation is free, but it is not cheap. For love is my most precious treasure. It is the only thing I take with me when I die while leaving my tired, ruined body behind. It is the only sustenance needed for eternal life with God.

Christ's death and resurrection did not end all suffering on Earth, but it provided a final means of escape from Earthly pain and suffering. The broken body dies, but in Christ, our soul lives. In Christ we will be without pain and suffering forever with God. Through Christ we are with the Father who loves us just as He loved His own divine incarnate mortal son, Jesus. John's Gospel repeatedly captures the words of Jesus on this,

> "If you know me, you will know my Father also... Whoever has seen me has seen the Father... Believe me that I am in the Father and the Father is in me... because I live, you also will live. On that day you will realize that I am in my Father, and you in me, and I in you." John 14:7-20

But do not misunderstand. I am still here, and my pain is not gone. My suffering remains. The darkness has not been overcome entirely by the light.

You do not turn on darkness, it's but the absence of light. Darkness turns on you and seeks to shield you from the light. The hardest part is reaching for the light and slowly pulling yourself into its presence where healing can begin and peace can be found.

In a world of light, there must also be darkness. How else would we know the difference? To know hope you must first know despair. It is in the darkness that you can finally see the light and claw your way back into its warmth. Reach for the light, and the light will reach for you.

Reaching for the light is an act of hope, proof that you believe in something more than yourself. Hope that engenders physical and spiritual endurance despite uncertainty and overwhelming odds. That I cry out from the depths of the abyss in search of light is itself proof of the Divine, for hope is embedded in my soul.

"All the darkness in the world cannot extinguish the light of a single candle."[3] – St. Francis of Assisi

In order to understand pain and suffering and why we struggle, we need to understand why we exist at all. Why does God create? This is a difficult question but an important one.

Why Does God Create?

If God exists, God is perfection. God is complete. God has no needs outside of His own greatness. So why would a perfect God create? God creates not out of necessity, not out of artistic expression, or in search of objective perfection, for perfection does not need practice. We are not a practice world among many draft worlds from which we were selected as the winner. No, the God of creation would create purposefully and perfectly the very first time.

I am not a biblical creation fundamentalist. I believe the universe is about 14 billion years old and the Earth is at least 4.5 billion years old. I do not date the Earth or the universe in accordance with the roughly six-thousand-year genealogy of the Bible or the six days of creation poetically described in Genesis. And I do not presume to tell God how to sustainably create.

Everything points to a God whose sole creative purpose is love. A God creator glorified through the love of what He has created. For if not love, then for what purpose? God lacks nothing that is material. God creates to manifest and share His glory. In other words, God creates out of sheer love for the purpose of love. But this is much more than romantic human love, more even than the love of a parent for their child.

Bishop Robert Barron describes God's love as the purest form of love. A love that exists only to will the good of the other. God's love is love that wants what is good for His creation, for us, not because it will benefit Him, but because it benefits us. God's love is more than selfless human love. God's love breaks all bonds of the ego. God's love is toward and for the other, humanity, even more than we can love ourselves.[4]

God's love is not just reflective. It is not just a mirror to the glory of God. God's love is expansive. God creates so that his love can grow. Love is the only thing other than God Himself that can exist in the absence of a receiver. And this is the heart of it. This is what makes God's love so special. God can create from nothing, and that creation can exist in a purely physical and material sense. But that creation has no purpose, for God needs nothing material or physical.

God freely creates out of love so that we can freely love. It sounds circular because it is. God can love me, but I am not required to love God back. That is my choice, and choice is at the core of what it means to love. Choice and love are the philosophical foundation on which everything else rests. When collapsed to its most basic level, the entirety of the universe and the purpose of our human existence is simply the canvas on which love can manifest for our benefit and for the glory of God.

God is the artist and paints our souls with love. Everything else in the cosmos is landscape, context, and background. They are not the purpose; they allow the purpose to exist. God effectively paints us with the light of His love. It is my choice whether I reflect that light back, glorifying God and connecting through that love with God. I can remain in darkness by absorbing all that light, all of God's love. Or I can reflect that love back to God and my fellow man in a rainbow of His glory.

Some will argue that this is human pride and ego selfishly making everything in the universe about us. But this is not what I am saying. I am saying the opposite. Because manifesting the purpose of our existence requires that we place God and the needs of our fellow man above our own. Lose yourself and you will find God. That is the core message of the Bible.

The guidebook to Heaven basically just says we already have the keys. To turn the lock, we need only to love God and love our neighbor more than ourself. Be like Christ, be selfless, the very opposite of human selfishness. It is so simple and yet so difficult. Thankfully we do not need to perfect selfless love in this life. We need only to practice it and strive to improve each day.

God can love us and all His creation perfectly and selflessly, precisely because He does not need us or our world. Humanity and the world add nothing to His greatness. God cannot tangibly gain from the world He has created. It is a widely accepted scientific fact that all that exists in the Cosmos today was present in the initial intense energy singularity of the Big Bang. God did not need it then, and He does not need it now.

God creates out of love for love's sake. God loves the world into being. He simply wills the good of the world. The biblical text in Wisdom is a metaphysical Godly truth.

> "For you love all things that exist, and detest none of the things that you have made, for you would not have made anything if you had hated it. How would anything have endured if you had not willed it?" - Wis 11:24-25

The fact that something exists means that it has been loved into being. Creation is not a one and done event. If something exists it is because God is continually willing that existence out of Divine love. Everything is a continuous manifestation of Divine love. That is how close we are to God. That is how personal our relationship is with God.

> "We love because He first loved us." - 1 John 4:19

Please don't misunderstand what I'm saying. The universe is not a windup toy created by God so that He can watch it run. The universe operates consistent with all the discovered natural laws of science. However, everything we see in the universe ultimately traces back to that initial moment of creation, the so-called Big Bang, that moment when out of nothing came everything. Just because we have deduced much of how the universe has unfolded from the moment of creation does not remove the need for a creator. The Big Bang still needs a "Big Banger."

We can never fully know God, but it makes no sense at all that a God of creation would then not be present in that creation. For God is not some artist that hangs his painting on the wall. If you are the God as revealed in Christ, there are no other Gods to share your creation with. To share your creation, you must remain part of that creation. You must remain present in that creation. The very presence that enables imperfect beings, man, to seek perfection in You and through You. This is the God of Christianity. This is the story of humanity that only God could write.

So often we depict God as a distant tyrant making these impossible moral demands on us, constantly judging our performance. If and only if we meet a certain high moral bar will God then take us seriously. But this is man creating limitations God has not, for if I can fully understand it, it's not God. And that is the point!

Do not reduce God to our human condition, for that is no God at all. God was nailed to a cross because we struggled with the mystery. The path to God is not lined with rules and procedures we will never get right; it is lined with love.

Spiritual life begins with the acknowledgment of the primacy of grace, that we have been loved into existence and all that is needed from us is to love God back. We are first and foremost spiritual beings. We are created from Spirit, from God, and we will return to Spirit. Our physical self seems all encompassing to us now, but our moral existence and our time here is just an instant of our spiritual existence, which like God, is eternal. We are not physical beings for the benefit of the physical, we are physical beings for the benefit of the spiritual. We are here to learn to love like God loves, unconditionally. I try each day to be a better person because that's an improvement that will last forever.

God is pure being and perfection, and very clearly my being and my mortal body are not. We should not take too literally the words in Genesis, where God said,

> "Let us make humankind in our image, according to our likeness." Gen1:26

The correct interpretation of the Hebrew text does not mean that God is in human form, but rather, that humans resemble God in their moral, spiritual, and intellectual nature. Paul describes this spiritual likeness in Colossians,

> "You have stripped off the old self with its practices and have clothed yourselves with the new self, which is being renewed in knowledge according to the image of its creator." Col 3:9-10

Humans are embodied with both an immaterial eternal soul and a physical temporal body, and while on this Earth the two are inextricably connected. Humanity is also connected spiritually to one another, to the natural world, and of course to God, the Divine, the Creator. While it is far too broad a topic to include here, the field of Quantum Mechanics, the physics of the fundamental subatomic particles and fields that comprise all matter and energy in the universe proves this universal oneness. Most scientists try to steer clear of the spiritual implications, but the connection between the physical and the metaphysical has been clear for almost one hundred years.

Louisa Gilder, in her book *The Age of Entanglement*, describes the distress the realization of quantum physics was causing its very authors. In her Chapter "Uncertainty – Winter 1926-1927," she quotes Nobel Prize winning physicist Neils Bohr in a strained discussion with fellow Nobel physicist Werner Heisenberg,

> "…you must understand the torture I am putting myself through in order to get used to the mysticism of nature."[5]

In a different conversation as captured by Timothy Ferris in his 1991 book *World Treasury of Physics, Astronomy and Mathematics,* Heisenberg says,

"Can you, or anyone else, reach the central order of things or events, whose existence seems beyond doubt... I am using the term 'soul' quite deliberately so as not to be misunderstood... I would say yes."[6]

What Heisenberg is suggesting is that at the fundamental quantum level we are all in some manner connected, and not just to each other, but to God.

Thankfully, God knows we are not capable of perfectly selfless Divine love and does not require us to achieve it. If we merely show one tiny spark of interest in God, God will come into our lives, invading us with His grace.[7] Where does all this lead? What does it mean to one day be with God?

In his *Summa Theologica*, Thomas Aquinas (1225 - 1274) writes in the very first section that the entire purpose of theology is to raise believers outside of and beyond themselves to a union with God who cannot be fully grasped. Aquinas argues that for an immutable reality, God, there can be no "before," "during," or "after." All God's being must be expressed, paradoxically, in an eternal, flowing now.[8]

If your being always was and always is, then the past and future are meaningless. God's being is always now! God was not a lesser God yesterday and won't be a greater God tomorrow. A perfect God is not being perfected. A perfect God, the God of Christianity, is always that immutable God: unchanging and unchangeable perfection.

God's eternity is not some everlasting duration. God is not a being who exists in endless, infinite temporal time to be endured. No, what St. Thomas Aquinas argues is that God is not in time at all. God is not long-lasting or short-lasting, neither fragile nor durable. The categories and measures of time do not apply to God because God Is not one of the realities in this world whose movement or transition can be measured.[9]

God is the only being that is both internal and external to this world, for God is forever both part of His creation, and by logical necessity as creator, outside of it. The canvas cannot form and paint itself. Only God is both essence and existence. To be God is simply to be. When Moses asked God for his name, there is a good reason God answered, "I am who I am." - Exodus 3:14

> "For as the heavens are higher than the earth, so are My ways higher than your ways, and My thoughts than your thoughts." - Isaiah 55:9

If we were to find God, to prove His existence, we would be sorely disappointed, for any God we could find would, by definition, have limits, and God does not. God is like the touch of the breeze on my cheek; I sense its presence just as it is gone. I feel its touch there, though I know it is everywhere.

God is intimately involved in every moment of our lives, but that doesn't mean that everything that happens is at His hand and part of His plan! Scripture tells us that there is not one sparrow that falls from the sky that God does not know and care about (Matt 10:29-31). But did God plan and execute that sparrow's fall, the tornado, the flood, or my cancer? No. This realization and the existence of human tragedy, of pain and suffering, leads many to doubt that the God of Christianity is truly a personal God, a God who hears our prayers and sometimes, according to His will, intervenes to alleviate pain and suffering.

Pain and suffering come from some physical or spiritual deficiency. God is perfection; therefore, God cannot suffer out of deficiency of His perfect being.

Yet, I believe that God does suffer with me. Not as I suffer, but because I suffer. God's infinite love for us means He suffers in love, like a parent who suffers when their child is in pain.

I don't doubt that God is manifesting a personal presence in our lives. My reasoning is simply that it is inconsistent that a God of creation would create and then not be present in that creation.

Yes, I could be wrong. But why would a God create out of love and then not be present in that love? There is an innate intimacy in this universe with the creator. Love is the reason we are here and the reason God is intimate here with us.

As Bishop Robert Barron has said many times and in many ways:

> "It is nonsensical to envision a God that can create from nothing, that creates for nothing."[10]

Having now addressed why a God of perfection would create, we must consider the next obvious question, a question mankind has been asking for thousands of years. Why would a perfect God not create a perfect world, a world without evil, pain, and suffering?

The Problem of Evil & Suffering

Armed now with a sense of the human struggle and some perspective on why a perfect God would bother creating, we need to consider the innate relationship between the existence of God and the existence of evil and of suffering. If we cannot reconcile the two, our faith is at risk of crumbling at life's first painful encounter. If this dilemma is not resolved before one of life's tragedies throw us into the dark abyss, we risk never getting back out.

Evil and suffering are both the absence of and the destruction of God's perfection. They represent a hole in what was once whole. Why do we concern ourselves with good and evil, joy and suffering? Why do we care? We care because we are moral beings, and as moral beings, we ultimately expect that there are compensations and consequences for good and evil. Pain and suffering are one of the main reasons humans search for meaning in their lives.

There are two kinds of evil in our world:

- **Moral Intentional Evil.** Bad things that humanity does to each other (war, terrorism, torture, etc.).

- **Natural Unintentional Evil.** Bad things that happen because we live in a natural world with natural forces and natural events (fire, flood, disease, death, etc.).

These types of evil can be related if man's activities, greed, and actions lead to natural disasters. But what I am interested in here and what I am suffering from is the consequence of natural, unintentional, and mostly random events that result in pain and suffering. In my case, a rare and aggressive cancer.

The way we experience and deal with suffering is highly dependent on our relationship with that suffering. For the cancer patient, the diagnosis is primarily emotional, with all that entails regarding pain, loss, purpose, and meaning. For the cancer oncologist, the diagnosis is primarily intellectual, leading to questions as to possible causes and treatment. The key difference is observing versus experiencing the consequences. The key difference is the extent of the associated pain and suffering.

Seemingly pointless suffering is often cited as proof that there is no God. But suffering is not of God. Suffering is because we are not God. We are not perfect.

If there is no God, then there is no intellectual justification for Good and Evil; and we are just creatures without souls, products only of our evolution, with no purpose and no innate moral standard.

If there is no God, then good and evil are meaningless. There is just life and death, the living and the dead. Life has no deeper meaning, and if life has no meaning, then what meaning has death? A meaningful life at least has the hope of a meaningful death.

The fact that we search for meaning from our suffering implies the existence of a moral arbiter, a moral lawgiver, a God. If we have an innate moral sense of right and wrong, then when we experience a tragic wrong, we search for its associated meaning and purpose. For if no God, why be outraged by evil and suffering? The lion does not apologize for eating the lamb.

On the question of evil, one is often tempted to simply state that we are not in Heaven but on Earth. And on Earth, without hate, what then is love? Without death, what then is life? A world where hate is possible is a world where evil is both possible and present. It is a world where freedom of choice is possible. We can choose to love and to hate.

A world of choice is a world where events follow natural laws, a world of possibilities and probabilities, a world of creation and destruction, of life and of death and of pain and suffering. In such a world there is uncertainty, and some randomness is present.

Human suffering has caused many to abandon belief in God, and so it is probably worth stating the obvious. There is lots of evil and suffering contained in the Bible, and never once does the Bible argue that they are incompatible with the existence of the loving God described therein.

Contemporary Catholic thinker and theologian Bishop Robert Barron has stated: "If human suffering undermines your belief in God, then, quite simply, you were not believing in the God presented in the Bible."[11]

The notion that a loving God could only be compatible with an absence of evil and suffering among humanity, the object of that love, goes back at least as far as the Greek philosophers and is first attributed to Epicurus (341-270 BC).

It is a simple argument, and it goes like this:

> P1. If an omnipotent, omnibenevolent, and omniscient God exists, then evil does not.
>
> P2. There is evil in the world.
>
> C1. Therefore, an omnipotent, omnibenevolent, and omniscient God does not exist.

Or, as stated by Epicurus,[12]

> "Is God willing to prevent evil, but not able? Then He is Impotent.
> Is He able, but not willing? Then He is malevolent.
> Is He both able and willing? Then whence comes evil?
> Is He neither able nor willing? Then why call Him God?"

It is a clear and at first seemingly valid argument. Indeed, if there is an all good, all knowing, all powerful, all loving God, why is there misery and suffering in this world?

Man has struggled for centuries with this apparent paradox. If I believe in an all-good God of perfection, then how can I explain evil, except to know that evil is not of God?

The most obvious problem with this argument is in the first premise (P1). While it is not entirely unreasonable that such a loving God would abhor evil, it is a considerable leap to also say that the two could not coexist.

There is, of course, the Christian understanding of evil and suffering which has already been alluded to. For love and joy to be possible, hate and suffering must also be possible.

There are some equally reasonable and plausible arguments why "evil" is a necessary component of the natural world. Is "survival of the fittest" in nature evil? Are the global weather patterns that scatter seeds on the wind and bring seasonal rains "evil" when a drought later occurs? No, they are consequences of a successful and sustainable planet Earth, in a solar system with a life-giving sun, existing within the broader viable universe.

Why didn't God merely create a world where tragedy and suffering do not exist? He did, at least allegorically. It was called Eden,[13] and we are not there.

Moral Evil

For all past and all future, God exists in a state of perfect love. God is not evil, and God does not create evil. If God did not create evil or death, where do they come from?

The Bible beautifully describes the gift of love and tells us clearly that love is the greatest, the highest value in the universe (1 Cor 13:13). To have a relationship with God, we must be able to experience love, but to give us the ability to love, God had to give us free will to decide whether to love or not to love. Why? Because love always involves a choice. Automatic or programmed love is not love at all. Like salvation, God's love is free, but it's not cheap! There are no innocent bystanders on the road to Heaven.

In a world without evil and suffering, could we truly know what love is? It is possible to exist in an all-loving world, but the absence of evil, hate and suffering would prevent us from knowing the alternative, and thus from making a choice to love. How can you choose good if you have no concept of evil? How can you love if you have no ability to hate?

We established in the preceding chapter that love is God's currency. The cost of love is evil. The consequence of evil is pain and suffering. Why is this? A world where only love exists is not impossible, but in such a world love is not a choice, it is a condition, for choice requires an alternative. Love that has no choice is no love at all.

For us to be able to experience love and to choose love, God bestowed on us free will. We have pain and suffering on Earth because we had the chance to live a life free of it in the biblically described "Garden of Eden," an existence with God, and we rejected it, at least allegorically. We sinned. With that sin comes distance from God and the presence of pain and suffering, as well as the knowledge of good and evil, and the ability to choose between them. To love one another and to love God, or not.

Either we have free will, the freedom to choose, or we do not. We cannot have it both ways. Whether you believe the Garden of Eden story literally or allegorically, in some way at some time, humanity made a choice. We cannot have a "do-over." Our world has evil, pain, and suffering, for it is a world where choice is possible. It is a world where our decisions affect our outcomes. It is a world where we can love and be loved, hate and be hated.

Granting free will to humanity means we are constantly faced with the choice to love self more than God, or to love God more than self. Yes, there is a correct answer.

It is important to understand that our choices do not change God. God's love is unconditional and infinite no matter what choices we make. That is the "God Deal." It does not mean what we choose has no impact on our salvation; it does. But our choices do not change God. God gave us a path through God incarnate, Christ, to one day again be free of sin and suffering. But that path is not easy. Choices have consequences.

Understanding precisely how the fall of humanity from the perfect presence of God to what is often referred to as a state of sin occurred is not so important. What is important is that there exists a Godly realm, which is indeed all good, and our human physical and spiritual being is no longer there.

Unfortunately, as recounted over and over in the Bible, and experienced six times in just the Book of Judges, we humans continually abuse our free will by rejecting God and turning away from Him. It is that rejection, what most Christians call an extension of original sin, that has resulted in the introduction of evil into the world, at least moral evil. Moral evil is the immorality, pain, suffering, and tragedy that occurs because we choose to be selfish, arrogant, uncaring, hateful, and abusive.

Apostle Paul writes:

> "All have sinned and fall short of the glory of God." (Rom 3:23)

So much of the world's suffering results from the sinful action or inaction of ourselves and others, but we choose how that story plays out.

"The only thing necessary for the triumph of evil is for good men to do nothing."[14]

You can choose to use your hand to hold a gun and shoot someone, or you can use it to feed the hungry. But it is inconsistent to understand God and love, and then to shoot someone and blame it on God for allowing the existence of evil and suffering in our world. As *Pogo* comic strip author Walt Kelly once wrote,

"We have seen the enemy, and he is us."[15]

Natural Evil

There is a second kind of suffering, called natural suffering or natural "evil," such as sickness and disease. It is an extension of what might be considered an evil of natural selection in the long process of perfecting lifeforms themselves, or natural "disasters" that are features of the working of the world around us. Some also see these as extensions of the corruption that "original sin" brought about in an otherwise perfect orderly Edenistic existence. I do not see it that way, and to argue this last point only raises the bar of plausibility for those who do not believe in a God.

Since it is not essential to either argument, I prefer to see such nature-driven "natural" events as conditions of the ongoing creation and destruction of matter and energy in the sustainable universe. Needless cruelty to another human or any creature is a manifestation of moral evil. Evil that has a choice. A disease that causes suffering and death, or an animal killing another animal so that one may eat and live, is not a moral evil.

We may not like certain inherent "cruelties" of the natural world we inhabit, and after a tragic earthquake or flood, we may be tempted to shout, "How then can there be a God?" But it is woefully inconsistent and illogical to blame God for not creating a more perfect natural world as part of the same argument that God does not exist.

As a meaning-seeking species, we tend to process events in terms of what they represent to us and how they fit into the "story" of our experiences. Our brains have a natural tendency to try to connect the dots, to find the point of a thing, for things must happen for a reason, they must have a point and be part of a plan. Our brains are not satisfied with randomness. "Why me?" and "Did I do something to deserve this?" are natural and common questions many people ask when faced with a sudden adverse event, such as a cancer diagnosis, the loss of a loved one, or a natural disaster.

For most of us, particularly those of us with scientific backgrounds, it becomes obvious that bad things happen in nature for the same reason good things happen in nature. They are subject to and driven by the same laws of nature that underlie all causes and effects. There is nothing special about the causes of "natural disasters," other than the fact that they led to outcomes that we humans judge to be "bad."

Therefore, the commonly asked question, "Why do bad things happen to good people?" is more logically stated as,

"Why would bad things not also happen to good people?"

This is particularly true when the cause of the "bad thing" is natural law or random mutation.

Time and time again, the New Testament tells believers that we will face persecution and suffering. The Gospel of James says to count it as joy when we encounter various trials (including persecution and suffering). Likewise, Paul tells us in Romans 8 that we are "heirs with Christ" provided we suffer with Him, and then he adds that the suffering of this present time is not worthy to be compared to the "glory that is to be revealed to us."

In other words, it is hard for us to see now, but the compensation for our suffering will be like the dollar we spent to buy a ticket that won the million-dollar lottery.

Even with all the reasons outlined above, we are human, and when faced with pain and suffering, we will likely ask why, and at the very least, like Jesus Himself in the Garden, we will ask, "Is there no other way, Lord?"

Too often our answers are insufficient. We say that we live in a fallen world, so we will certainly face the effects of that fallen existence. That is true, and it is the answer I mostly use myself. But I do not think it is the whole story. It is a case of necessary, but not sufficient.

While it explains the existence of imperfection, it does not fully explain the intended purpose of suffering. And in our tireless search for meaning, we seek that purpose. We see in the New Testament that suffering is not just a reality, but a reality with a purpose.

Like the athlete who suffers pain to build strength and endurance, a Christian suffers the same way but for spiritual strength and endurance. These are skills needed to compete and win the battle against the darkness, the Not God, Satan (if you must give it a name). Now I do not like the name Satan, or Devil, or the childish images they often evoke, and so I use it here only for convenience. I hopefully know even less of Satan than I know of God, but for me, Satan is simply the absence of the light and the love of God. God is the light. The Not God is the dark. The "Dark Side" of all that is good in the universe.

As believers, we have only two choices when faced with suffering. We can draw nearer to God or push God away. And if we push God away, what does that say of our faith? Sometimes our faith fails us in our struggles because we have fallen victim to the "Prosperity Ponzi."

The Prosperity Ponzi

We love God **not** because we have been given much and have never suffered but because of who He is.

I am a "Believe It to Receive It" Christian, but I am not a "Name It and Claim It" Christian. These are not just two sides of the same coin; they are different currencies meant to purchase different treasures.

When someone learns of my cancer and then asks what I had done to deserve it, there is a good chance they have been listening to one of the prosperity preachers. They are usually on TV in huge stadium-like churches. They are good-looking, have perfect smiles, wonderful families, beautiful homes, fancy cars, and a jet airplane. They preach the "prosperity gospel," in which God grants health and wealth to those with the right kind of faith. The obvious implication is that those who do not have health and wealth must have done the wrong thing, prayed the wrong way, practiced the wrong kind of faith in the wrong kind of God, or a combination of all these deficiencies.

It is not that God does not want us to be healthy and wealthy, He does, though we should be careful with the definition of "wealth." It is not a tit-for-tat deal where I pray and believe in the right way and God will ensure I have earthly health and wealth. As the wonderfully candid Mother Angelica once said on her TV talk show,

> "God is not a slot machine. We do not go to God to get something; we go to give something."[16]

Paraphrasing one of the more reasonable prosperity preachers, Joyce Meyer, "Who wants to wait until Heaven to be healthy, wealthy, and beautiful?" I admit that I also sometimes enjoy listening to Joyce Meyer and I respect her for posting a video on

Instagram, on January 7, 2019, where she admits to getting some of the prosperity theology wrong, saying,

> "I'm glad for what I learned about prosperity, but it got out of balance… every time someone had problems it was 'cause they didn't have enough faith. If you got sick, you didn't have enough faith. If your child died, you didn't have enough faith … Well, that's not right. There's nowhere in the Bible where we're promised that we'll never have any trouble. I don't care how much faith you've got, you're not gonna avoid ever having trouble in your life. Jesus said, 'In the world, there will be tribulation. Cheer up, I have overcome the world."[17]

Hearing a prosperity preacher admit they got it wrong was big news for me. Still, many will continue to sell the promise that if we pray right, Heaven will come to us on Earth. This depends on one's definition of Heaven.

> "But strive first for the Kingdom of God and His righteousness, and all these things will be given to you as well." - Matthew 6:33

"All these things" are the earthly necessities of food, clothing, and shelter, but they are noted as secondary to the Kingdom of God, for,

> "Is not life more than food, and the body more than clothing?" - Matthew 6:25

The point being made by Jesus is to put spiritual matters first.

> "I am the bread of life. Whoever comes to me will never be hungry, and whoever believes in me will never be thirsty." - John 6:35

Jesus makes it clear He is the living bread of life, and through Him spiritual thirst and hunger are defeated forever. Shortly before this Jesus clarified the treasures of His kingdom.

"Do not store up for yourselves treasures on Earth, where moth and rust consume... but store up for yourselves treasures in heaven... For where your treasure is, there your heart will be also." - Mathew 6:19-21

Yes, Jesus said many times, "Ask and you shall receive." But the caveat was always to "pray in Jesus' name," - John 14:14, or to ask "according to His will." - 1st John 5:14

Those who follow the prosperity preachers and believe in God's promise of physical wealth and health in this life will eventually be disappointed. Christ's whole message consistently emphasized that His kingdom is not of this life, not of this Earth, so why would He value earthly treasures?

These are treasures of man, not of God. For God, the only treasure is love and it is to be given away so that it may be received.

If you want belief in God to fail you, then fail God in your belief.

The one great consistency of God's message, of the God story, is that it is never the story as man would have written it, hence its inherently convincing authenticity. The whole point of the new covenant established by Christ for man is that the new temple is Christ Himself and the new kingdom is eternal, and therefore not of this earthly domain.

It only makes sense that God is little concerned with material wealth that has no value to Him who has all, or even to us if our focus and our purpose is seeking to join Him. The only currency that transcends our mortal to eternal existence is love and that is why it is the only currency God accepts. Any theology that seeks to justify a view of God and faith as a means to earthly gain clearly has read a different Bible or surgically taken small sections of the Bible completely out of context, such as here, where Jesus says,

"So, I tell you, whatever you ask for in prayer, believe that you have received it, and it will be yours." - Mark 11:24, and

"If you abide in me, and my words abide in you, ask for whatever you wish, and it will be done for you." - John 15:7

The key "prosperity gospel" message is to pray as if we have already received, and in doing so, God has no choice but to manifest that reality. It is a dangerously self-centered faith that puts me and my needs at the center and asks God to deliver or prove that He is no God at all. That is exactly not the Christian God.

It is a case of, "If I truly believe it, then I will receive it," with no consideration of the appropriateness of the "it." The prosperity gospel is more a case of,

"If I only pray the right way then I get to play the right way."

While belief is indeed almost synonymous with faith, any man that seeks to threaten God even subtly will eventually be surely and sorely disappointed.

"You ask and do not receive, because you ask wrongly, in order to spend what you get on your pleasures." - James 4:3

As we see later, earthly health and wealth are not the rewards received by any of Christ's most devoted servants. We are to pray in praise of God's glory, not to seek our own glory. If you collapse the "prosperity gospel" down to its core, that core is man. The core is man's ego. And in doing so, man becomes master and God is reduced to servant, a "genie in a bottle" attending to our needs.

The "prosperity gospel" is essentially just another Ponzi scheme, stealing from the not yet spiritually disappointed to recruit the not yet materially anointed.

When we say, "Pray beyond your wants and receive beyond your needs," it does not mean when $100 is needed, ask for $1,000 and receive $1,000,000. It means, pray for more than yourself and your earthly wants and you will receive beyond your needs for all eternity with God. For,

"Happiness is found not in what you possess, but in what possesses you."

The fallacy of focusing on earthly treasure is that happiness is never found there, for you will not find happiness without holiness. In order to find God, you must first lose yourself. The best thing you can do spiritually for your ego is to let it go. The "prosperity gospel" is all about ego, and you will find little good about ego in the Bible.

These words of George MacDonald say it perfectly,

"If we do not die to ourselves, we cannot live to God, and he that does not live to God, is dead."[18]

I can see the appeal of the "Prosperity Ponzi" if we think of God anthropomorphically, as an extension of man, some "Superman," but with at least some of man's imperfections of being. A god reminiscent of the Greek gods. An angry Zeus. A jealous Aphrodite. Such a god who views us as too small and unimportant to love, or a god that views us as perhaps relevant but too commonplace to bother with. These are human emotions. Why would we think these are Godly emotions?

Faith most often fails us when we put God in a box of our own construction. We then absurdly look for Him there, and yell, "See, there is no God," when He is not found. Alternatively, in our egotistical rejection of beliefs or morals that get in the way of our nihilistic obsession with pleasure and possessions, man effectively kills God, so as to make man god. A case of God is dead; therefore, I am God.

"Deus est mortuus, ergo ego sum deus."

This is the basis of the societal relativistic moralism that is increasingly popular today. A belief system that has no moral absolutes, but rather defines acceptable morality as whatever society is willing to tolerate. A form of "do no harm" morality where the definition of "harm" is constantly changing.

This truth about our right relationship with God is at the heart of the Bible Book of Job, a book all about underserved suffering. Satan asks Job whether he loves God purely, without reason or the promise of God-given reward. The question is, does Job love God simply because He is God, or because of what God can do for him here on Earth? Satan sets out to prove Job, a man who had everything, had fallen for the Prosperity Ponzi.

Satan speaks to Job and accuses him of loving God only because he has been richly blessed. He says that if God would take away such blessings, then Job would curse God and cease to love Him. The undertone of Satan's argument is that Job's love of God, and by extension, our love of God, exists only because we have never suffered.

Yes, Job once had everything, but then Job suffered horrifically, again and again. He suffered unfathomable moral and natural evil. He was tortured and humiliated. He lost his family and all his possessions. It is hard even to read, let alone to have lived it. But Job did not recant. He did not blame or abandon God. Job suffered and still loved God.

And in the end, after great suffering, God rewarded Job, not by restoring all that Job had lost, but by entering his life, embracing him, and loving him. This repudiates Satan's main argument, that humanity only loves God when we experience the gifts of a gospel of material abundance and joy.

But I have suffered, we have suffered, and we, like Job, can repel the darkness of frustration, sadness, and pain. We can defend ourselves with proof against the "tit-for-tat" lie of Satan. Satan tells the story as only man would tell it. A story of selfishness, hate, blame, revenge, jealousy, and despair. God writes the story only God could write, one of selfless sacrifice, tireless love, blameless forgiveness, and eternal hope.

It is often our suffering that strengthens our spiritual armor against Satan's darkness, the terminal and interminable absence of God, a horror that goes well beyond Gustave Doré's image of *Dante's Inferno*.

> "Totally without hope one cannot live. To live without hope is to cease to live. Hell is hopelessness. It is no accident that above the entrance to Dante's hell is the inscription: "Leave behind all hope, you who enter here." - Jürgen Moltmann[19]

Is our suffering all part of God's plan, or is it intrinsic to our fallen human existence?

Gustave Doré 1857   Public Domain

Pain is Not God's Plan

Is my cancer, my pain, and my suffering, all part of God's plan for me, one tragic event on a set day of my tragically predetermined life? No, for if my life was all predetermined, then I am not free to choose, free to impact events in my life. If our world was a clock and God the clockmaker, then there is no free will, no choice and no good or evil, just mindless automation in a world wound up and set to run.

The clockmaker could love the clock, but the clock could not love the clockmaker. Such a world is not our world because I know love and I know hate; I know good and I know evil. These are not randomly acquired constructions of an overactive brain for the benefit of my human comfort and existence. These are aspects of my soul, which transcends the natural because it comes from the supernatural. There is an expected relationship, an exchange between us.

And as now stated several times, the currency of that exchange is love. I can withhold it, or I can share it; it is my choice. The more I give it away, the more I have. It is not of this world alone, it is the currency of transcendence to more than this world, to more than this existence. God only asks that we freely spend our love as the price to break the bounds of this finite natural world and live on with Him forever.

So no, God did not give me cancer. Just because God is all powerful does not mean God is all doing, the divine puppeteer, and we the mortal puppets. God is involved in everything, but God is not controlling everything.

God is the source of all beings, but our human existence is outside of God's perfect being so that nature plays out "naturally" and we can exercise our free will. In allowing freedom in His creation, God gladly gave up a certain degree of His power to control us. God is a loving parent, not a puppeteer.

God's perfect will is life and love, joy and wisdom, and beauty and truth. These are of God; they are good and are part of God's Will. When evil happens, it is not part of God's Perfect Will, it is part of God's Permissive Will. God does not cause evil, but God permits evil; He allows it to happen.

In the Sermon on The Mount, Jesus says of his Father,

> "For He makes His sun rise on the evil and on the good, and sends rain on the righteous and on the unrighteous." - Matthew 5:45

What Jesus is saying is that some rain will fall on all lives; God does not discriminate regarding who receives what from the natural systems of this world. Good or bad, you will experience both the sun and the rain, the effects of which are also sometimes good and sometimes bad.

Think of it this way: God has created the perfect stage and made rules for how man should act on that stage. But it is man who writes the script and acts out life, either abiding by the rules or not.

To reiterate my point, your loss, your pain, and my cancer are NOT part of God's plan. He allowed them to happen, but He did not cause them to happen. Our suffering is not God's intent, it is a condition of our imperfect human existence which God accepts.

"God weeps with us so that we may one day laugh with him." - Jürgen Moltmann[20]

I believe I have done mostly good in my life, but I am a perfectly imperfect human. I do not "deserve" my cancer, and I am not being punished. I believe if I was being punished, I would know and know why. Because God created a world where He is not the puppet king, where He is not in control of every little thing, bad things happen. But God could heal me and take my pain and suffering away, and He may yet.

God knows that even amid the worst evil, pain, and suffering, He can bring about a greater good. God did not want Jesus to suffer and die. God allowed it to occur, knowing that by doing so, great things would happen. God became human, He became vulnerable, and we killed Him, leading to the greatest event in human history; even in that very act, when we killed God, when we killed selfless love and goodness incarnate, God turned that evil into our very salvation.

It is true, He died at our mortal human hands so that we could live and share immortality with Him. It is crazy, and that is why I know it's true. Humans do not think or write this way. Even when evil happens, it does not thwart God's plan. We will dig deeper into the purpose of pain in the next chapter.

I may be broken, but God washes His love over me like water and a rainbow appears in my soul. God knows that He can take this broken thing and make it whole again.

The Broken Rock Falls photo shown below was taken by a friend at the very time I was secretly struggling to write this.

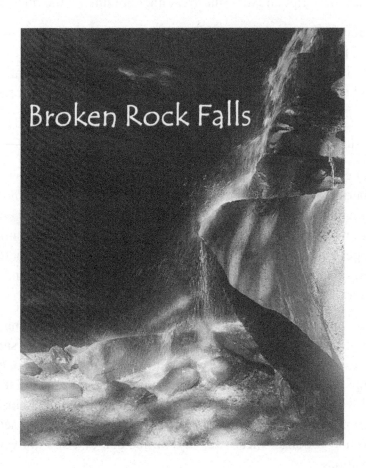

She sent it to me with this note:

> "We took a trail to Broken Rock Falls, and at the bottom was a rainbow… My mind went right to you. Our lives are at times broken, but we can hold onto God's promises! For me it was a reminder that God always has us, He is always with us. That is what the rainbow said to me." (I am sorry the beautiful rainbow isn't visible in the black and white printed image.)

The Purpose of Pain

It was the great C.S. Lewis who wrote in his book, *The Problem of Pain,* one of his most famous lines:

> "We can ignore even pleasure. But pain insists upon being attended to. God whispers to us in our pleasures, speaks in our conscience, but shouts in our pains: it is His megaphone to rouse a deaf world."[21]

And as St. Augustine wrote in his 5th-century book *The City of God*:

> "God wants to give us something, but cannot, because our hands are full, there's nowhere for Him to put it."[22]

Most of us are guilty of carrying our God parachute around, only deploying it when we are helplessly hurtling toward the ground. It's there for emergencies and we hope we'll never have to use it. While our life remains agreeable to us, we will not surrender it to God, or at least not fully, the way God wants us to. Lewis describes this problem, writing,

"I call this Divine humility because it is a poor thing to strike our colors to God when the ship is going down under us; a poor thing to come to Him as a last resort, to offer up 'our own' only when it is no longer worth keeping… but He will have us even though we have shown that we prefer everything else to Him, and come to Him because there is 'nothing better' now to be had."[23]

Image by brgfx on Freepik

And this surrender is not as a slave to deeds but as a slave to God's love and our love for God. That we have enjoyed a good life is not the sufficient insurance we need for eternity. Pain shatters first our human illusion that all is well and second our illusion of self-sufficiency. A case of: "Give me pain so that I may know thy gain."

The fundamental Purpose of Pain is to get our attention. This is true physically and spiritually. Physically it's why we pull our hands away from the fire. Spiritually, pain helps to pull us toward the light of God. Pain humbles us. Pain creates urgency in cultivating our relationship with God so that it will be there to save us when our ship goes down.

God speaks to us; we have only to listen. Apostle Paul suffered tremendously throughout his ministry, and Paul speaks of a "thorn in the flesh" in 2nd Corinthians, where he writes:

"Three times I appealed to the Lord about this, that it would leave me, but He said to me, "My grace is sufficient for you, for power is made perfect in weakness." So, I will boast all the more gladly of my weaknesses, so that the power of Christ may dwell in me. Therefore, I am content with weaknesses, insults, hardships, persecutions, and calamities for the sake of Christ; for whenever I am weak, then I am strong." (2nd Cor 12:8-10)

Many explanations have been put forward as to this "thorn in the flesh," and we will never know for sure, but the interpretation I like the most is that Paul was asking for relief from his chronic eye disease so that he could better write and preach the gospel. That God saw a better good in Paul's suffering than from his healing is a hard message, but it helps me to bear my own chronic illness. If I was not suffering, I would never have written this book. It is a salve to my wounds.

God is mostly concerned about how our life on Earth prepares us for our life in Heaven. It may seem that God cares little of our suffering "here," for he knows it will end "there." We are in "God's Training Camp." The fact that God already loves us does not detract from God's purpose, which is to make us more lovable, though not how we define lovable, but how God defines lovable.

C. S. Lewis in his classic 1952 book, *Mere Christianity*,[24] says that by becoming human, Christ "infected" humanity with His spirit and that man's continuing struggle to become more Christlike is the sole purpose of Christianity. We are to first practice at being better than we are so that we can gradually become better. There is a cost to this improvement, which is often more than we have anticipated.

Lewis compares it to God entering our human house, and like a moral handyman, he begins to make improvements. At first, we understand the little things here and there that God is fixing, but then He begins to knock down walls and renovate us in ways we did not anticipate or want. He does this because He intends to come live within us, and we become a room within His house. Christianity is not about mere improvement; it is about transformation. Lewis acknowledges that our starting point on the spiritual journey is not so important as the choices we make along the way and whether we finally give ourselves over to God.

The purpose of evil, pain, and suffering in this world is not solely to humble us so that we can open ourselves to God. But it is a key purpose. Sometimes only in our darkest moments can we truly hear God, to accept and come to know God. It is in the darkness that we can best see the light of God, and then come to love, trust, and commit ourselves to God. Our suffering matures us, grows us spiritually, and makes us more Christlike.

But to follow Christ is not simply to imitate him, for becoming Christ is impossible. Nor does it mean some cultish hero worship. The way each of us follows Christ is to carry our own cross while following the mission of Christ in our daily lives, a mission made clear in the Gospels.

God also reveals Himself to us in suffering in ways that we could otherwise never have known. My cancer changed me in ways I was otherwise unlikely to undertake. I am not thankful for my suffering, but I am grateful for what it has revealed to me.

The point, as I understand it, is not to search for meaning in when or why tragedy has occurred, but to search for meaning in what we can do about it.

What else am I to do? On one hand, I have my suffering but also my love, hope, and the promise of a world where only undamaged bodies have risen from the dead to share eternity with Christ. On the other hand, I still have my suffering, but with no transcendent love, no hope, and no promise of the perfected presence in Christ with the Father forever.

Given this choice, my decision is easy. My decision is simple yet complex beyond our understanding. I choose God and I ask Him to help me on the rest of my journey to Him, for if the journey was easy, then what is the need of God? Why do we struggle so much with this? Because it is a God Deal, a God thing, a thing so far from our human limitations that we cannot accept the boundless love and grace of God that it so freely provides. As the great 17th-century thinker Blaise Pascal once wrote,

> "If I believe in God and life after death and you do not, and if there is no God, we both lose when we die. However, if there is a God, you still lose and I gain everything."[25]

We should never minimize our pain and suffering; it is very real. But it helps if we take a long-term perspective, an eternal life perspective. A teenager who had spent more of his life in the hospital than out of it once said beautifully:

> "I suffer greatly now, but God has all eternity to make it up to me."

In Romans, Paul writes:

> "I consider that the sufferings of this present time are not worth comparing with the glory about to be revealed to us." - Romans 8:18

And remember, Paul suffered countless beatings, stonings, imprisonments, rejections, hunger, thirst, and finally martyrdom. Yet Paul says,

> "For this slight momentary affliction is preparing for us an eternal weight of glory beyond all measure." - 2nd Cor 4:17

And John wrote,

> "Jesus said: 'I have said this to you, so that in me you may have peace. In the world you face persecution [trials & tribulation]. But take courage; I have conquered the world.'" - John 16:33

God offers us the two things we need when we are hurting: peace to deal with our present and courage to deal with our future. Why and how? Because God, through Christ, has conquered the natural world! Through Christ's own suffering, death, and resurrection, He has deprived this world of its ultimate power over us. Suffering does not have the last word anymore. Death does not have the last word anymore. God has the last word!

 At the heart of Christianity, there is the cross. What is an all-powerful God doing on a cross, the very icon of pain, humility, and suffering? What does this reveal to us about the problem of pain? It tells us this God that became man, God incarnate, God and man, is not distant from us.

It says God has Himself become part of our natural world, subject to evil, pain, and suffering. Only God could defeat what comes to all natural things - death. Only God could bring back to Him what He loves and that which seeks and loves Him, such as us. He did this by rising from the dead. God completed the covenant with man and authenticated the promise of loving Him.

If Jesus did not rise from the dead, then Christianity would have died and still be dead. If Christ's resurrection and our salvation are not true, then I have only my pain and suffering, and they have no purpose. But there is purpose, for it is true that Christ did rise.

The Truth of It All

If man's thirst for meaning, for justice, for good over evil, for God, if this was all a delusion, a conspiracy of comfort, a Marxian "opiate of the masses," what did its early conspirators gain from their efforts? There was no earthly glory or wealth for any of the early Christians. What was the purpose for them to devote and sacrifice their lives to spreading this new Christianity? What did any of the early Christians have to gain from perpetuating a Christ Conspiracy? Nothing. Christianity survived then and survives now because it is true!

If the Old and New Testaments of the Bible and the life, death, and resurrection of Jesus Christ are all a conspiracy, then what an incredible conspiracy it has been. A conspiracy involving hundreds of thousands of key participants spanning well over two thousand years of prophecy and fulfillment of prophecy, all perpetuated without any clear reward for those involved. Quite the opposite, the early pivotal participants in this "conspiracy" were poor, beaten, jailed, and then martyred for their beliefs - beliefs that afforded no advantages on this Earth.

What other selfless cause in human history comes even close to it in magnitude? There is just no plausible basis for the fabrication of a conspiracy on this level, let alone sustaining the conspiracy over generations. As Sophocles said over 2,500 years ago,

"A lie never lives to be old."[26]

Even short-lived conspiracies need a purpose and a reward. Where is that purpose? What is that reward? No, all conspiracies of man throughout history have been constrained to a few individuals, short-lived and selfish in their objectives.

The bigger delusion, the much more unbelievable story, is that Christianity was created by man for man. Christianity only makes sense if it came from God for man. Without this, there is no hope for anything in or beyond the pain and suffering of this world. For while the atheist also has pain and suffering, by definition, he tragically has no hope.

Hope is at the heart of the purpose of pain.

"Hope is the art of seeing something more there when there is nothing more here."

As to the scientific plausibility of the resurrection, it is important to understand that if we could understand miracles, they would not be an act of God. Must we, as the atheists insist, be able to describe in great scientifically repeatable detail how resurrection could occur within the laws of nature as we know them and then be able to demonstrate it experimentally? It is illogical that our standard of proof would be that we must be able to do the very thing we are in awe of God doing.

Perhaps it is simply too obvious to even point out that the very being that designed the natural laws, set them in motion, coexists within and outside of those laws as their Creator, would not be subject to their constraints in the execution of a miracle. Certainly, I cannot perform any miracles, which is precisely the point. If there is a God, then by definition, that God is more than we are. Is it impossible to believe that a God of creation, who is present in that creation, cannot also operate within that creation in ways that appear miraculous to us?

The resurrection is not just some event that we factually decide is true or false and then move on. When we decide Christ's resurrection is true, it is that acceptance and affirmation of the truth that changes us. Because Christ still lives, He invades us with His spirit and we carry Christ with us as our guide in this life and into the next.

So where do we draw the line between what is possible and impossible? We draw it at religious belief and call it faith. To believe in God is to believe in more than what we are now, it is to believe in what we can become. Our beliefs guide us, our faith strengthens us, but our love, our love feeds our spirit now and forever.

This God of Christianity, Jesus Christ, God incarnate, has risen from the dead and has said in His own brief ministry that He will be the moral judge, and as both God and man, He is going to judge fairly and absolutely. This says that the Hitlers, the Pol Pots, the Stalins, and other terrorists will not ultimately get away with it.

This is both comforting for our moral sense of vindication and yet equally frightening, given how far we are from living the life of Christ. And here is the uniquely Christian God-given genius of it: The Christian message tells us that we can face that judgment because God assures us that He will offer each of us the opportunity of forgiveness in this life, not because of what we have done, but because of what Christ has done on our behalf.

The secret of our relationship with God is that it's not a merit system; it's a union and it is unconditional. Thankfully my wife married me with the promise of love in good times and bad, for richer, for poorer, in sickness and in health, and she took that promise and union seriously. She loves me, and I love her. I am far from a perfect man or perfect husband, but like God's love, my wife loves me despite my imperfections. I do not have to earn that love each day. And likewise, my love and acceptance of my wife does not depend on proving merit. Unmerited love is true love, and God has shown us the way.

Forgiveness? I only need to ask for it and love the God that freely gives it to me. This is Godly Grace and only God can give it. How does it help with this problem of suffering? It helps because if this is true, then it changes everything. I believe it is both true and consistent with all that we have discovered of the natural world around us and of what God has revealed to us of Himself and God within us. God promises us that the death we fear is not the end. He tells us that our pain and suffering are not the end.

There is more to come, and that more is a place with God, a place without pain and suffering. That is huge.

God has solved man's suffering by suffering as a man. He vindicated His love for us through the validation of His very humanity. He suffered. He died. I only need to love Him to share in His resurrection.

But for many, the relief of suffering in this life will only come in the next. The challenge is, can I trust God with the messy mystery of faith? If my alternative is atheism, which I do not believe works intellectually and which, by its very definition, provides no transcendent hope whatsoever, then my answer is an unequivocal "Yes."

After I have taken in all that I can, after I have reasoned with all my mind and searched with all my heart, I trust the Christian God with my life, my death, and my resurrection in Him and with Him.

But the problem remains. To what extent is pain and suffering a necessary part of this journey back to God? Why do some equally good people suffer terribly while others do not? That is a difficult question, and we discuss it further in the "Let Go! Let God!" chapter, but it is something we will never fully answer in this life.

Perhaps it is as simple as random chance and the fact that a functioning society also needs healthy people to care for those who are not able to care for themselves. If some benchmark of pain and suffering was required of everyone for their salvation, it would change the God Deal described earlier. The God Deal is not based on my merit. It is not based on my earning a place with God.

For those of us with poor health, the explanation might be as simple as a case of bad luck. God did not set me up for failure while he set another person up for success. Life happens, death happens. God is concerned about how we respond to our challenges as we encounter them.

There is no proof that I am right to trust in God. There is no proof that I am wrong. But I am comforted that people who have repeatedly experienced suffering see in this message a doorway into hope because they know God is not only a God of love, but He is also a God of compassion and compensation.

Yes, something will come of my pain and suffering. It will be of God and with God. Who am I to judge its sufficiency, to weigh the cost of my pain and suffering to be in the presence and the glory of God? If we could see that reward and compensation for our love and faith purified in the fires of our suffering, we would have our proof. But again, that is not the God Deal.

We must trust now in the proof that only comes when we reach our destination. We must invest in our spirituality now for dividends to be paid later, for we can only know for certain the value of suffering in this life after we have gone to the next life, where there is no more suffering.

> "Perhaps God remains invisible so that He may know who sees."

The Old Testament is full of suffering as man progresses through a series of evolving and always broken (by man) covenants between God and His people. But God does not play with man in an endless malevolent cycle of sin, suffering, repentance, mercy, and deliverance. The struggles of man in the Old Testament provide a necessary foundation and maturing so that we may receive the coming of Christ.

Think about the context of Christ and the new and final covenant without the context of the many failed covenants of the Old Testament. One of the best arguments for the validity of the Christ story of Christianity is that while truly epic and legendary in its proportions, it is just too radical a story to be authored by man, it is a story only God could write into reality, and it is why we are still talking about it and believing it today!

The Apostle Paul understood that Israel's role, the role of the Jews, the people of his heritage, was not as an exclusive and elite society of God's people, the "God Club." Rather, Paul understood that Israel was the means by which God had laid the foundation for Christ's saving grace for all. Israel was not God's chosen people because they were the only people who God cared about; they were God's chosen people to demonstrate that the Law is never enough.

For centuries, God's foundation people had been instructed in the Law, but they repeatedly failed to keep it. The Law is not itself a path to salvation and the eternal God. Those who did keep the Law, like Paul himself, abused it by condemning others who were not in their Jewish God Club, a club they had corrupted. The expansion of God's Ten Commandments into the 613 laws in the Torah, the first five books of the Hebrew Bible, is an example of a man hopelessly trying to codify God and, in the process, corrupting faith. Paul is special because as a Pharisee he was of the Law, and by his own admission, he was never fulfilled by it. Paul says,

> "Therefore, the law was our disciplinarian until Christ came, so that we might be justified by faith." - Gal 3:24

Paul was explaining that the purpose of the Law was to bring a man to Christ by showing him that by himself, he was utterly unable to keep the Law, God's Law. The Law simply reveals man's need for more! The Law puts us on the path to God, but we'll never get there without Christ and God's Grace!

Sin, evil, and suffering are not "of God" but arise from a rejection of God, a rejection where one chooses to satisfy their ego over the greatness and goodness of God. Is it any surprise that human sin and suffering line the path back to that same God? If all humankind were lovely, worthy souls, a people of angels, there would be nothing extraordinary about God's grace.

And that is the problem. When we elevate ourselves and our worthiness, we make God smaller than He is by undermining and belittling the wonder of God's grace toward us. To minimize the wretchedness of man is to minimize God, for admitting the depth of our unworthiness gives us the first real glimpse into the enormity of God's unfathomable love for us, the enormity of our God, one of the great mysteries of faith. I am a very unworthy soul, and my God is indeed a very big God.

While it is beyond the scope of this book to include it here, the evidential basis for belief in an Intelligent Designer of our universe is almost overwhelmingly compelling. However, to believe in the radical, incredible, unfathomable scope of the infinitely loving God revealed to us by Christ, that is where mystery and faith come in.

In today's egocentric "Me World," we sometimes mistakenly think Christ's death proves our worthiness. It is because we are not and can never be worthy of God's grace, of God's everlasting embrace of our soul, that the sacrifice of the truly worthy, the Christ sacrifice, is proof of a God we are born searching for but can never fully understand. I believe there is much truth in the realization that:

- "I fully understood God when I realized God could never be fully understood."
- "Any God that I can truly… fully… know, is no God at all."

The Passion of Christ screams at us from the pages of the New Testament, screaming far more than pain and suffering. The screams are not of a cruel God but are screams of God's love for us. The pain, the suffering, and the sacrifice of Christ as a man are what made us pay attention, the end of which reveals the depth of God's love.

That our human imperfection and unworthiness to know God is perfected freely in Christ is a gift of mercy and love only God could conceive. God's only requirement of our worthiness is to recognize our unworthiness. We only have to believe in the gift to receive the gift.

Only God could make "free" the greatest gift of all.
Only God could do the God Deal, and a huge part of the God Deal is to help us to move beyond our pain.

Moving From Pain to Gain

God always gives us what we need, though not always what we want.

The phrase "No pain, no gain" is often referred to in physical activities but is even more valuable when referencing spiritual strength. In addition, my pain and suffering may help not only my spiritual growth, but the spiritual growth of others.

There are fundamentally only two boxes into which we can place everything we do in our lives. These boxes are:

- **Satisfaction** - serving our own needs, desires, and pleasures
- **Sanctification** - self-sacrifice, serving others, and placing others' needs before our own

These boxes are not mutually exclusive, as sanctification can also provide satisfaction. The converse can also be true, although much less likely.

Everything we do in life serves at least one of these and eventually leads to a choice, as in the sacrifice of self-satisfaction for the purpose of sanctification. We are not talking here about asceticism or extreme abstinence of physical needs and desires. Joy and happiness are not only okay, but they also reflect God's love and beauty in us. But life presents challenges, and faith in Christ allows us to see every challenge as a way of achieving some aspect of our sanctification.

It was St. John Vianney who said:

"The greatest cross is the fear of crosses."[27]

"We cannot escape from it… Why not love our crosses and make use of them to take us to Heaven? If we could but go and pass a week in Heaven, we would know what this moment of suffering is worth."[28]

I know personally from my recurrent cancer that when we fear the cross, we carry it twice. If we can conquer fear, we can put on the armor of Christ's love. This requires mindfulness to live in the present moment and not dwell on the past or fear the future. We cannot sanctify the past or the future; we can only sanctify the present by embracing the cross in the present.

Christ carried the heaviest cross on our behalf, and while He may not take our cross away, He assures us that He will help us carry it, and more importantly, He has given us the promise that even our heavy cross has a purpose.

That purpose is the presence of Christ with us as we struggle with physical and mental pain and suffering, and the hope it does not end here. With Christ, the finish line shifted from this world and this life. With Christ, our finish line is with God. And I believe it with the certainty that we can believe anything, that Christ will be there with the Father welcoming us across that finish line into their presence forever. A forever with no pain and no suffering. No longer the human struggle of sanctification, but a sanctified presence with God.

If I give myself to God like He gave Himself to me, my life is safely in His hands. If I truly trust in this, I can be less focused on living here, now, on Earth; and recognize that which I so fear is not the end, but truly it is the beginning.

Daniel Glauber Pixabay.com

There may be nothing more challenging in this life that we will ever do, but if we can learn to embrace our pain and suffering for the good it provides, then we will no longer fear it, and when the fear is gone, the anxiety of future pain and suffering is also gone.

The irony of this is that what we fear, the suffering of the cross we bear, is also the answer to our fear. To lose our fear we must embrace it.

All humans experience anxiety, and we have only two options to defeat it:

1) We satisfy the anxiety, the craving, the hunger, the fear. We eliminate or consume the very thing that has caused the anxiety. However, if we cannot eliminate or remove that thing, our only choice is,

2) We embrace it and learn to love the thing that we once feared. Embracing the thing you fear and the thing you hate is deeply difficult and only a selfless God-like love will give us the strength to successfully and sustainably do it.

Our mortality and sense of impending loss underlie most of our fears. When this fear, including fear of death, leaves us, we are free of the destructive ego-driven anxiety accompanying it. We are then able to move from anxiety to serenity.

It may seem more than ironic, even impossible to comprehend, but loving the thing we fear the most, the thing at the root of our anxiety, and embracing the good in it, however hard that is to see or feel, yet trust in Christ that it is there, our embrace squeezes out the fear and shields us from the anxiety.

We are left with peace, serenity, acceptance, and only the good. Others that love us may still feel the anxiety, but that is not proof of our failure; for us, it is gone. Their battle remains, but in winning our battle, we help them to win theirs.

I hate my suffering and I do fear death, but I have learned that hating it does nothing to remove it, in fact, it makes it worse by reinforcing its presence in my mind and in my life. There is nothing natural or human in the statement "Love your suffering and it will set you free." Doing it is even less "natural."

The love to do this derives not just from our minds and our mortal bodies but also comes from the selfless, unconditional, unending love of God. And by receiving and directing that love toward suffering and the very thing in our mortal human world and existence that seems the most unworthy and unreasonable, will we begin to defeat it. If you see Divine love and the presence of Christ in all things, you become one with the body of Christ. We don't suffer as Christ or for Christ, that redemptive work has already been done for us. But, when we embrace our suffering, we join Christ in its defeat.

> "As you, Father, are in me and I am in you, may they also be in us… The glory that you have given me I have given them, so that they may be one, as we are one" – John 17:21-22

It is not what man would do, it is what God would do; it is what God did, in Christ, on the cross. Sometimes God makes it so simple we cannot do it. How do we liberate the power of the Lord?

I did not sign up to be a saint, and I am lousy at sanctification. I did not send my life's resume to God with a message, "Please choose me for suffering, Lord." And I do not believe God did choose me to suffer. I suffer because I am a mortal being in a mortal world. With very few exceptions, the person that has not suffered has not lived.

I suffer because a cell randomly mutated within my body and created cancer. My cancer is a rare sarcoma that predominantly and cruelly strikes the otherwise very healthy and active among us. Whether I was genetically more or less predisposed to such an event is not important. All that is important is that it happened. I could have been hit by lightning, maimed, or killed by a terrorist or a tornado. When bad things happen to good people, it offends our sense of fairness, and we ask, "Why me?" or "Why them?"

But, as noted earlier, perhaps the more appropriate question is, "Why not me?" or "Why not them?" Trying to come to terms with the full extent to which randomness rules our lives and our lack of control over such things is pointless because even if we knew, we could not change it. If it could not happen, we would be living like a cog in the clockmaker God's clock.

Like light and dark, if good has meaning, so does bad. We make things difficult for ourselves by dreading that very thing. If we can learn to welcome the discomfort, by surrounding it in love, it has no power over us. Dread, anxiety, and fear just make our eventual journey back to the light longer and harder. And yes, because we are human, sometimes we will falter, but we must keep trying, for when we let go of worthiness we let go of "worriness."

And this brings us to The Power of *Irrational Hope*!

The Power of Irrational Hope

When the path ends where you do not want to go, find joy in the going.

It can be hard to love when pain and suffering have taken so much of what you treasured in this life. Yet, no matter your situation, love remains, for it is the only treasure even our mortal death cannot steal. With love, there is huge upside and no clear downside. Is it even possible to love too much? Love is God's currency, and He wants us to spend all of it, for the shortest path to joy is the one littered with love.

At its core, all hope is anchored in the divine promise that this life has meaning and that there is more than this life. Without the connection to the divine, hope is nothing more than ego-driven emotional support for a future better than the present. Mortal hope falls far short of divine hope, precisely because it is mortal. And like all mortal things, it eventually runs out. We search for meaning in our lives only to find out one day the meaning is the search.

Divine hope is possible because of Christ's resurrection, but it is not just about struggling through this life because we know it's better in the next life. Divine hope takes the realization of everlasting life and manifests that joy now, every day, in this life. Knowing we will be with Christ in death allows us the joy of Christ in our life now. The very essence of hope is Christ in our life.

It is very hard, but in searching for hope, even *Irrational Hope*, it helps if we stop complaining. Complaining dwells on the darkness, the negative, and hinders our ability to go toward the light, the positive. Complaining has no redeeming benefit, and unfortunately the more we complain, the better we get at it. The more we complain, the more we will suffer, because it prevents us from reframing our situation toward the positive.

Reframing is the opposite of complaining. We must constantly strive to reframe all we struggle with into our love and faith in God.

"If we can be cheerful when fearful, we can turn our worst day into our best day."

Complaining is subconscious atheism and walls us off from within ourselves. Complaining shuts off the search for good, the search for divine assistance, the expression of love, and the sense of shared suffering with Christ. Complaining is a glimpse of hell within us. The "Not Godly" us. And studies have demonstrated that complaining diminishes our immune system and increases our risk of infections, disease, and yes, even cancer.

Irrational hope is only irrational when embedded in this world where our logical mind assesses it as unlikely and unreasonable given our knowledge and experience. The late TV talk show nun, Mother Angelica, once described it this way,

"Unless you are willing to do the ridiculous, God will not do the miraculous. When you have God, you do not have to know everything about it; you just do it."[29]

God has proven He can do the impossible and often did what to man was irrational. The Gospels are mostly filled with Jesus doing the opposite of what we as humans expected Him to do. Our faith in God and what He can do must be like the child who does not know unicorns don't exist.

German theologian Jürgen Moltmann calls this the,

"Passion for the possible."

Moltmann is saying we must not limit ourselves only to what is possible for man. He defines a new possibility in Christ, saying,

"In the medium of hope our theological concepts [the resurrected and returning Christ] become not judgments which nail reality down to what it is, but anticipations which show reality its prospects and its future possibilities." [30]

For if we limit what God can do to what we can do, then what purpose is faith? To fight our natural, doubting, complaining nature, we must reframe and prepare our response before the next trigger even comes. In that way, we have already decided how we will behave. As writer James Baldwin puts it,

"Not everything that is faced can be changed, but nothing can be changed until it is faced." [31]

Disappointment and sadness may not be totally avoided, but they are no longer a destination. They must become a trigger for greater glory in the suffering that each time reveals more of God to us. It seems impossible, and it is when we try to do it alone. Jesus said,

"I will not leave you orphaned [comfortless]; I am coming to you." - John 14:18

We need to have this image of the higher good firmly in our mind. It is like a net that prevents us from falling back into sorrow and despair. Our anxiety comes from a negative processing bias in our brain, and it takes tremendous effort to stop it, but we must stop it, even if we cannot yet achieve a positive bias.

When our brain perceives a threat, it secretes adrenaline to prepare us for our response. When we reframe that threat from negative to positive, we shift the adrenaline away from the negative physical dread to the positive spiritual peace, where God is in control. Our adrenaline then helps us manifest positivity and joy rather than sadness and fear.

This is the establishment of a virtuous cycle, where even another setback or challenge helps to support my illumination of God and my loving community with God. I know, it seems impossible. But most of us know someone who demonstrates this ability to always see the light, even in near-total darkness. They have proven it is possible.

Like Jesus, we must strive to become dangerously unselfish, to find God in all things. To demonstrate an attitude of gratitude, even when we suffer. The point is, you must *act* positively, as any attempt to think positively will fail. Why not make today the day you want tomorrow to be? Choose to be happy and find joy in all things.

God's participation in our human suffering is not only key, it is the key. By suffering and dying as man at the hands of mankind, Christ showed us both our innate sinful rejection of God as well as the infinite love and mercy God has for us. Man's sinful crucifixion of Christ was turned upside down to become the undeserved act of man's redemptive salvation. But there is a catch. To receive that salvation, we must believe in Christ's death and resurrection. We must accept by faith what God has freely given us.

When we speak of suffering and of trusting hope, we must never forget that even Jesus, fully human and fully Divine, felt the anguish of what was to come in His crucifixion. Jesus asked God the Father if there was any other way to redeem the sins of man. In the Garden of Gethsemane, just before Jesus was arrested, He prayed to His Father saying,

> "My Father, if it is possible, let this cup pass from me; yet not what I want but what you want." - Mat 26:39

> A little later, Jesus prays, "My Father, if this cannot pass unless I drink it, your will be done." - Mat 26:42

The "cup" to which Jesus refers is the suffering He was about to endure, and when Jesus petitions the Father, "Let this cup pass from me," He expresses the natural human desire to avoid pain and suffering. Jesus is fully God, but He is also fully human. His human nature, though perfect, still struggled with the need to accept the torture and shame that awaited Him. Jesus was battling the flesh and its desire for self-preservation and comfort.

The struggle was intense. Jesus said,

> "I am deeply grieved, even to death." - Mat 26:38

And Luke the physician observed that Jesus was "sweating blood," a sign of extreme anguish (Luke 22:44). Jesus loves mankind, but His humanity dreaded the pain and sorrow He faced, and it drove Him to ask His Father if it was possible to avoid what was to come. In the Garden, Jesus conquered the flesh and kept it subordinate to the spirit. This was hard even for Jesus - no wonder we often fail at it.

When we face trials, it's good to know that Jesus is aware of what it's like to want God's will and yet not want it; to act purely out of love yet dread the pain that often follows; to desire righteousness and obedience, even when the flesh is screaming out against it. This conflict is the inevitable collision of our humanity with our spirituality. We are not Jesus, nor are we saints. Let us pray our cross is one we can carry knowing that although I am helpless on my own and cannot do it by myself, God always can.

The doctors have no more treatments for my cancer. From their perspective, I am "terminal," meaning "cancer that cannot be cured and eventually leads to death." In the world of mortal men, there is no hope for my cancer-free recovery. I clearly understand that any further hope for the medical healing of my cancer is indeed irrational.

But my hope rests not in man, but in God. With God, human scientific irrationality has no meaning, for God is not limited by what man can do. Irrational Hope is the expectation of the possibilities of what God can do, based on what He has done!

Irrational Hope is only dangerous when it causes us to act irrationally. I would not leap off a tall building hoping I could fly. Some have criticized faith as a form of Irrational Hope. However, my faith in God is both rational and evidential. My belief in God is scientifically compelling based on arguments too extensive to include here, including the incredibly fine-tuned nature of the world around me. Even concerning the resurrection, the factual and circumstantial evidence is very strong. For me, faith in the resurrection is required only because, as humans, we don't know how to do it. After all, it's a God thing, which is precisely the point. For me,

"Irrational Hope becomes rational when you include God."

The very nature of hope is the expectation of the possible, and as such, it is always forward-looking. Hope for something in the past that has already occurred is not only irrational but also nonsensical. Hope is about the future. That is why we need it.

Even if our now is pain and suffering, hope provides a future without it. Without hope, we die, for why prolong misery only to have more misery? While they do not call it Faith or admit to its spiritual nature, even an atheist who persists in pain and suffering demonstrates hope.

It is crucial to understand that Irrational Hope and the handing over of control to God does not guarantee we will be healed or spared from our suffering. For a miracle is a God thing on God's terms. The ministry of Jesus told us this about a relationship with God where miracles can happen.

- Miracles are the visible glory of God expressed as love for the perfection of his creations.
- To engender a Miracle, we must replace fear with Love.
- Prayer is the medium we use to communicate our love for our Creator.
- In prayer we speak from our hearts not our minds.
- A miracle is the spiritual self in union with God conquering the physical self.

I may not be blessed with a miracle, but what we can be certain of is that all things are better when done with God, particularly pain and suffering.

Success in this life is not about the path you took, but how you took the path. Trusting in God is the path to the other side. How do we better trust God? We Let Go! And we Let God.

Let Go! Let God!

If we want to change our mood, we must change our thoughts. Our thoughts become our mood, and our mood frames our reality, our acts, and our activity. I must act positively in order to think positively. If our sadness buries our thoughts and prevents the foothold of hope, then we must act our way back into hope.

Actions that do not support our thoughts are like interference on the radio, making it hard for us to hear the music. Likewise, having a positive attitude will help me to think positively. If you do not feel positive, pretend your way back into the light. We need to Let Go and Let God![32]

This does not mean avoiding responsibility for our actions and our thoughts. It simply means that when we struggle to do it on our own, we must let go of control and let God help us.

> "Cast all your anxiety on him, because he cares for you." - 1 Peter 5:7, and

> "Now to him who by the power at work within us is able to accomplish abundantly far more than all we can ask or imagine." - Eph 3:20

Do not do what we typically do, which is to be anxious about almost everything, and to pray about almost nothing. Rather, pray about almost everything and be anxious about almost nothing. Try to do this each day by imagining two boxes. One is an Anxiety box and the other is a Prayer and Thanksgiving Box.

Frame your thoughts in the following way:

Anxiety Box → Put Nothing

Prayer & Thanksgiving Box → Put Everything

As Paul says in Philippians,

> "Do not worry about anything, but in everything by prayer and supplication with thanksgiving let your requests be made known to God." - Phil 4:6

When you finally realize you cannot carry the weight of all your Earthly challenges by yourself, you finally realize who can. It is the essence of the Let Go! Let God! mantra of Alcoholics

Anonymous. Only by submitting to God do we receive God's strength. In the words of Jesus shared earlier,

> "Are you able to drink the cup that I am about to drink?" - Matthew 20:22

Here we are presented with one of the most profound truths of Scripture. God does not ask us to do anything that Jesus was not asked to do and did.

Yes, we endure hardships, persecutions, and suffering, but Jesus, as man, also endured these. He can understand and empathize with how we feel better than we can imagine. But the task is not easy, for I am not Jesus and I am no saint.

> "Then He [Jesus] said to them
> all: 'If anyone would come after
> me, let him deny himself and
> take up his cross daily and follow
> me. For whoever would save his
> life will lose it, but whoever
> loses his life for my sake will
> save it.'" - Luke 9:23-27

Our own suffering does not save us. Instead, we are saved by the suffering, death, and resurrection of Christ. Our own suffering is merely an opportunity to participate in Christ's suffering so that one day we will share in His glorification.

> "We suffer with him so that we may also be glorified with him." - Rom 8:17

As Christians, we can expect some suffering in our lives, but must we all suffer to be saved? Those who can consistently and sincerely put others and Christ first in their lives (without the focus suffering provides) may be blessed to avoid physical pain. However, their focus on others and their unity with Christ means they will experience emotional suffering. All we know is that those who suffer are more readily able to put earthly ego and possessions aside and seek comfort and joy in Christ. The always insightful St. Thomas Aquinas explains it this way:

> "For the merits of [Christ's] Passion to be applied to us, we need to cooperate by patiently bearing the trials God sends us, so as to become like Christ."[33]

Pope John Paul II reaffirmed this in his Apostolic Letter Salvifici Doloris (1984):

> "In bringing about the Redemption through suffering, Christ raised human suffering to the level of the Redemption. Thus, each man, in his sufferings, can also become a sharer in the redemptive suffering of Christ."[34]

Pope Paul implies that our suffering not only supports our salvation in Christ, but that like Christ, our suffering can further benefit and support the salvation of others.

In coming into our world, God entered our space and time, He entered our suffering. Even sadness with one you love is better than joy in isolation - if such joy is even possible? That is the truth of true love. It is only because you have deeply loved that you can ever deeply grieve. God's presence in our suffering is the same. In the Bible, Job is satisfied with God's presence, even though God gave him absolutely no answers to his tortured suffering.

Out of our tears, our waiting, our darkness, and the agonizing isolation of our very soul, Christ comes into that darkness and shines His light. The hand of God is always there, always reaching for us, we only need to reach for God.

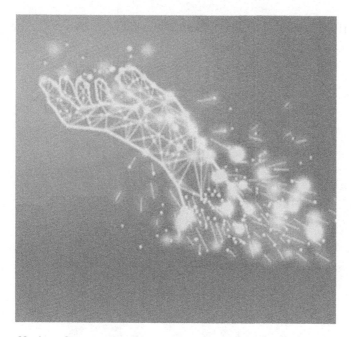

After suffering from radiation, chemotherapy, and many cancer surgeries, I am increasingly less fearful of death, but what I fear is dying. I fear the path, not the destination. However, I am comforted that my suffering will not be more than I can endure.

"No trial has come to you but what is human. God is faithful and will not let you be tried beyond your strength; but with the trial he will also provide a way out, so that you may be able to bear it." - 1 Cor 10:13

Never give up hope, for hope is God, and God never gives up on us. We do not need to do it alone. But for this to work, we must develop a personal relationship with God. There is no right way and wrong way to do this. Treat God like a friend, speak to him daily, and ask for his help and presence in your life. When we feel the battle is lost, we must fight on our knees, with the "sword of the spirit" and God at our side.

We must be careful not to use our pain as an excuse not to live. We have a community of loving souls, a "Community of Saints" around us. Many have suffered, or will suffer, as we suffer. Many have suffered more. All seek victory in Christ. We need them in our lives.

We carry our cross on a road surrounded by those who love us, who pick us up when we fall, quench our thirst, and light up our souls with their own.

Weeping along with me is the therapy I need. If you share even just an understanding of my suffering, you will help lighten my load. When we act kindly, it also gives meaning to our own lives, as we see that we matter to others.

"Spend your love wildly in this life, so that you can be sure to have enough to last forever."

Heaven is More Than Enough

A successful Christian is not someone who has solved the problem of suffering, but one who has faced the way the world is, and despite this reality, has come to love and trust in God.

I have never found the sidewalk "Repent and you will be saved" preaching either convincing or effective marketing for the conversion of nonbelievers. It is not because I doubt the need to acknowledge our sins and ask God for forgiveness. It is because I believe the unbounded, unconditional, and unimaginable love of God for all of us is the message we all need to hear and the meaning we all seek.

When we feel God's love, we also feel our own imperfections and contributions to human pain and suffering, and we accept our accountability and ask for forgiveness. Even more importantly, we trust in Christ for that forgiveness and the promise of a world where there will be no more suffering.

Again and again in scripture, the joys of Heaven are presented against the suffering on Earth. A Heaven that is More than Enough. But Heaven is not our payment for suffering; it's not tit-for-tat. Heaven is being in the eternal presence of God and surrounded by all the unimaginable glory of God, where there is no suffering.

The well-known John 3:16 verse offering eternal life to all who trust in God can be frightening when our current lives are miserable. What if eternity is also misery? But that fear completely misses the point. Eternal life is not an infinite extension of this mortal life, and it is not simply an escape from this world.

This life is but the introduction. We are not meant solely for this world. Eternal life is with God, the God embodied in Christ and freely shared with all believers in Him. As our mortal lives unfold, they lead us ultimately toward radical transformation in union with

God. A resurrected, transfigured, and transformed life in the glory of God.

Mortal death is part of God's providential design; a design where we are ultimately drawn into real union with Him. We are destined for a life more than this world, a life with God, for as author Wayne Dyer and several others have similarly said,

> "We are not human beings having a spiritual experience. We are spiritual beings having a human experience."[35]

Many today are embarrassed to talk about Heaven, as our delusion will surely draw snickering from others. But I do not have childish Sunday School image of Heaven as some shining city in the clouds where God sits upon His golden throne.

The best descriptions of the spiritual realm are given by those who through their own Near-Death Experiences (NDEs) can uniquely share their enlightened vision of life and death. The topic of NDEs is itself too vast to cover here, but there are many credible experiences as related by medical professionals themselves. Two excellent starting points are the book *Proof of Heaven* by neurosurgeon Dr. Eben Alexander and the video interview with Deborah King, Johns Hopkins ICU nurse and later a Dr. of Clinical Psychology available on YouTube (https://www.youtube.com/watch?v=eH3-WZWEMqY).[36]

In addition, in the past twenty years there have been many peer reviewed studies in the medical journals on NDEs. Of particular note is the large-scale study of cardiac arrest survivors by Dr. Pim van Lommel as published in *The Lancet*,[37] the work of Dr. Sam Parnia as published in the medical journal *Resuscitation,*[38] and the books and articles by Dr. Charles Greyson, Professor Emeritus of Psychiatry and Neurobehavioral Sciences at the University of Virginia.[39] Finally, you can visit the website of the International Association for Near-Death Experiences which has been in operation since 1981. (https://www.iands.org/)

While in this world, and short of having my own Near-Death Experience, I cannot know what this otherworldly Heaven truly is. I must be satisfied knowing what Heaven is not, and in Heaven, there is no pain and no suffering. For me, Heaven is a state of endless Joy in the glorious loving presence of God. If that is delusional, then all of Christianity is indeed delusional and false.

Fortunately, just because something is helpful does not make it false. Because something is innately desired does not make it delusional.

If I am delusional about my faith and am wrong, I have lost nothing. If on the other hand, as the atheist believes, there is no final accountability for our actions, no true moral authority, no God, and they are wrong, they have lost everything.[40]

A Harvard Medical School study of cancer patients in the Boston area, a part of America not particularly high in religious attendance, reported that 84% of patients affirmed that religion was helping them cope with their cancer diagnosis, and religious coping closely correlates with a higher quality of life.[41] If we are delusional, at least we are in good company.

Time after time throughout human history, societies turn to or away from religion and God based on their level of societal security. The decline of active, practiced religious faith in Europe mirrors precisely the post-WWII sustained peace and prosperity coupled with the increase in societal security through universal healthcare and social welfare. In every study across the globe, lower societal security leads to higher religious beliefs and values, and vice versa.

The Bible describes this in countless examples, with one of Jesus' most famous statements:

> "Again, I tell you, it is easier for a camel to go through the eye of a needle than for someone who is rich to enter the kingdom of God." - Matthew 19:24

We may not need to experience pain and suffering to enter the Kingdom of God, but we do need to recognize it as an opportunity to find a unique union with Christ that makes entry easier. And all we can be sure of regarding Heaven is that it will be far greater and far more glorious than we can imagine. We do not know what heaven is, but as monk and spiritualist, Father Thomas Merton once said,

> "Well one thing's for sure - there sure won't be much of 'you' there."[42]

Merton said this to the novice Father James Finley during the time he was Finley's spiritual mentor. The story, as told by Finley, is that one day he sought out Merton to ask him about something that had been deeply troubling him. He was concerned with this whole matter of death, life after death, and resurrection. Finley piously asked Merton,

> "What do you think happens to us after we die?" and, "What do you think about the Kingdom of Heaven?"

Finley relates that Merton, with a twinkle in his eye, burst into laughter and responded with his famous, "Well, one thing's for sure, there sure won't be much of 'you' there!"

Finley says he slowly came to understand Merton's unexpected response. It was meant to shatter the pious self-importance of the young novice before him. Merton was saying that Finley's human sense of identity and importance all needed to die and was, in fact, going to die. He was telling Finley to get over himself, for the best way to get to Heaven is to leave yourself behind![43]

Mother Angelica put it this way,

> "You can't go to heaven full of pride and say move over, Lord, I've got a better idea."[44]

We spend much of the first half of our life searching for who we are and much of the second half trying to put who we are aside so that we can better know God.

But how do we live in Christ so that Christ may live in us? As Jesus clearly puts it, one "self" must die for another "Self" to be born. That message is quite explicit in all four Gospels (Matthew 16:25; Mark 8:35; Luke 9:24; and John 12:24). We must stop smothering our spirituality with our humanity. To be with Christ, with God, we must push our ego out of the way. For eternity is a long time, let us be sure to spend it with God, and,

"If your life is Hell, make sure your death is Heaven!"

Epilogue

Thank you for allowing me to share my spiritual journey, my faith, and my beliefs with you openly and honestly.

Writing about what I have learned during my own struggle with pain and suffering has helped me to accept and understand its purpose, and I hope this book will help others in a similar way. I do not claim that all my interpretations of these Godly mysteries are correct, for we each must seek truth based on our personal relationship with Christ. It is only in Christ that we find the promise of *Irrational Hope*, the knowledge that with Him all things are possible.

I thank God for the friends and family who have stood by me throughout my battle with cancer. You helped me find the light when I was lost, and you lifted me up more than you can know.

Love and peace of Christ to you all.

Robert Ryan,
May 2023

About the Author

Robert (Rob) Ryan has long been a curious soul cursed with thinking a bit too deeply about things. Rob's mother often shared the story of picking him up one day from a church preschool when he was four years old. On the drive home, his mother asked, "What did you do in school today?" Rob responded, "We learned stuff about God." His mother said, "And what did you learn?" Rob replied, "We learned that God always is." He then went on to say, "And that's okay, but what I don't get is how God always was."

He was raised Catholic and attended a Catholic school through the eighth grade. In 1981 he graduated *summa cum laude* from Ohio Northern University where he studied science and engineering. Rob never took his faith on faith alone and he has spent many years studying physics and metaphysics for rational and evidential answers to life's questions.

First diagnosed with a rare sarcoma cancer in January 2016, Rob has been through six major surgeries, radiation, chemotherapy, and immunotherapy. He still battles his cancer every day and though he may yet be blessed with a healing miracle, Rob knows his struggle has brought him closer to God, and that God has all eternity to make up for the suffering in this life.

When not writing, traveling, or being treated at MD Anderson Cancer Center, Rob spends time with his wife, Vicki, at their homes in Texas and Michigan or visiting their children in Chicago and Geneva, Switzerland.

Author's Favorite Lines

(All can be found in the book.)

- Time weighs most on those who have it least.

- I wish to spend my remaining time on living, for death needs none of it.

- When I base my hope on the possibilities of what God can do, the irrational becomes rational.

- My love is both the only currency I have, and the only currency God accepts.

- My salvation is free, but it is not cheap.

- In a world of light, there must also be darkness, how else would we know the difference.

- That I cry out from the depths of the abyss in search of light is itself proof of the Divine, for hope is embedded in my soul.

- Lose yourself and you will find God.

- God's love, perfect love, is love that exists only to will the good of the other.

- God freely creates out of love so that love can be freely created.

- There are no innocent bystanders on the road to Heaven.

- I am a "Believe It to Receive It" Christian, but I am not a "Name It and Claim It" Christian.

- If you want belief in God to fail you, then fail God in your belief.

- The "prosperity gospel" is essentially just another Ponzi scheme, stealing from the not yet spiritually disappointed to recruit the not yet materially anointed.

- Happiness is found not in what you possess, but in what possesses you.

- You will not find happiness without holiness.

- In order to find God, you must first lose yourself.

- Success is not about the path you took, but how you took the path.

- To believe in God is to believe in more than what we are now, it is to believe in what we can become.

- Hope is the art of seeing something more there, when there is nothing more here.

- Our beliefs guide us, our faith strengthens us, but our love, our love feeds our spirit now and forever.

- Perhaps God remains invisible so that He may know who sees.

- I fully understood God when I realized God could never be fully understood.

- Any God that I can truly fully know, is no God at all.

- When we let go of worthiness we let go of "worriness."

- When the path ends where you do not want to go, find joy in the going.

- Love is God's currency, and He wants us to spend all of it, for the shortest path to joy is the one littered with love.

- We search for meaning in our lives only to find out one day the meaning is the search.

- If we can be cheerful when fearful, we can turn our worst day into our best day.

- If we limit what God can do to what we can do, then what purpose is faith?

- Why not make today the day you want tomorrow to be?

- Irrational Hope becomes rational when you include God.

- All things are better when done with God, particularly pain and suffering.

- Success in this life is not about the path you took, but how you took the path.

- It is only because you have deeply loved that you can ever deeply grieve.

- When we feel the battle is lost, we must fight on our knees, with the "sword of the spirit" and God at our side.

- We carry our cross on a road surrounded by those who love us, who pick us up when we fall, quench our thirst, and light up our souls with their own.

- Spend your love wildly in this life, so that you can be sure to have enough to last forever.

- Never give up hope, for hope is God ,and God never gives up on us.

- We must stop smothering our spirituality with our humanity.

- Eternity is a long time, let us be sure to spend it with God.

- If your life is Hell, make sure your death is Heaven!

Images

1. Cover Image – Created by Delos Studio specifically for the book.

2. Hands with Science & God Puzzle Pieces: Author edited image from freerangestock.com, photo by RACOOL, #4792

3. Man & Whirlpool: Author created image from Free Use Image by Naomi Booth, Pixabay.com combined with Deposit Photos Image 492470664 and Image 427172948; purchased and licensed for use; www.depositphotos.com

4. Man Reaching from Depths Toward the Light: Author created image from Deposit Photos Image 70476057 by Dmytro Tolokonov and Image 592954906 by Samul Ponce, purchased and licensed for use; www.depositphotos.com

5. Gustave Doré 1857 Public Domain Print: Image is from Gustave Doré's 1857 illustrations for *Dante's Inferno*. Title: "The Thieves Tortured by Serpents," engraving illustrating Canto XXIV of the *Inferno*, verses 89-92; http://www.gutenberg.org/files/8789/8789-h/images/24-233.jpg

6. Clockwork Man on Earth Torso: Author created image from freerangestock.com, "Earth with Tree between Hands" and "Abstract Person with Cogwheels," photographer Jack Moreh, #2728

7. God is No Puppet Master: Author created image from freerangestock.com, "Manipulative Person – Manipulative Boss," Image by Jack Moreh, #2728

8. Broken Rock Falls: Photo by Armstead, taken at Broken Rock Falls, Hocking Hills State Park, Ohio, USA.

9. Man with Hands Full: Public Domain Clipart, https://freesvg.org/vector-illustration-of-man-trying-to-carry-too-many-boxes

10. Sinking Ship Illustration: Image by brgfx on Freepik, https://www.freepik.com

11. Hands Embracing Suffering: Author created image, Hands Image from "Clker-Free-Vector-Images" on Pixabay, https://pixabay.com/vectors/hands-two-open-silhouette-welcome-296850/

12. Cross: Clipart Vector from Pixabay, https://pixabay.com/vectors/christ-christianity-cross-jesus-149313/

13. Carrying Cross: Author modified illustration from Deposit Photos, Image 247285526 by Marinka, purchased and licensed for use; www.depositphotos.com

14. Hold on To Hope Card: Author modified image of card created by Armstead.

15. Hands Holding Fear: "Fear Embrace Clouds" Image by Pixabay, by Daniel Glauber, https://pixabay.com/illustrations/fear-embrace-clouds-sky-hands-772516/

16. Smiley Face on Face: Author created image from freerangestock.com, "Tablet Showing Sky Over Face," photographer Ed Gregory,

https://freerangestock.com/photos /40267/tablet-showing-sky-over-face.html

17. Choose Happy Image: Author photograph of unattributed artist image on purchased wood block accessory by Giftcraft, Fabricator's Name: Jiujiang Ivzhouyuan Wood Industry Co. Ltd, 8/2021

18. Believe It to Receive It Image: Author photograph from a church in Europe.

19. Prayer & Thanksgiving Box: Author created imaged from freerangestock.com, by Kaboompics, https://freerangestock .com/photos/78263/photo-details.html

20. Reaching Hand: Author created image from freerangestock.com, "Digital Transformation Concept - Hands Reaching Together," Jack Moreh, #2728

21. Hugging Tree with Cross: Author photo, Michigan, USA, 2022

22. Heaven Image: Author created image, "Clouds Heaven Boat" image by Gerd Altmann, Pixabay, https://pixabay.com/ illustrations/clouds-heaven-boat-sea-water-waves-808749/

23. Author Image: Author created image from photograph.

Endnotes

---

[1]Francis Bacon, *Advancement of Learning,* (1605), The 1893 edition pub by Cassell & Co., London, is available at: https://www.gutenberg.org/files/5500/5500-h/5500-h.htm

[2]*The Pentateuch,* By Michael D. Guinan, (Eugen, OR: Wipf and Stock Publishers, Aug. 8, 2003), Ps 69, p. 52, previously published by The Liturgical Press, 1990, The specific Bible version used for this choice of text is not specifically attributed, but it is the text used in the Catholic Mass Responsorial Psalm on July 13, 2021. Also Available at: https://www.thegospelforyou.com/jesus-speaks-of-judgment-day/

[3]St. Francis Of Assisi, *The Little Flowers of St. Francis of Assisi,* by Ugolino di Monte Santa Maria, ed & trans by W. Heywood, (New York: Vintage Spiritual Classics – Random House, May 1998),

[4]Bishop Robert Barron, "You Have Been Loved Into Being," Sunday Sermon, *Word on Fire,* (Oct. 29, 2022), Available at: https://www.youtube.com/watch?v=qg5nOSDSMyc

[5]Louisa Gilder, *The Age of Entanglement: When Quantum Physics Was Reborn,* Chapter 12, "Uncertainty – Winter 1926-1927," (New York: Vintage, 2008), p. 101

[6]"Werner Heisenberg, Positivism, Metaphysics, and Religion" in *World Treasury of Physics, Astronomy and Mathematics,* ed by Timothy Ferris, (New York: Little, Brown and Co., Jan 1, 1991)

[7]Ibid

[8]Thomas Aquinas, *The Summa Theologica of St. Thomas Aquinas (revised ed.), translated by Fathers of the English Dominican Province. – via New Advent.— Summa Theologica*, (Complete American edition, 1920), Available at Project Gutenberg

[9]Ibid

[10]Bishop Robert Barron, "You Have Been Loved Into Being," Sunday Sermon, *Word on Fire,* (Oct. 29, 2022), Available at: https://www.youtube.com/watch?v=qg5nOSDSMyc

[11]Bishop Robert Barron, "Should Suffering Shake Our Faith," *Word on Fire*, (April 13, 2021), Available at: https://www.wordonfire.org/articles/barron/should-suffering-shake-our-faith/

[12]Numerous references to Epicurus at: https://en.wikipedia.org/wiki/Epicurus#Epicurean_paradox

[13]See "Garden of Eden." In Abrahamic religions, the Garden of Eden or Garden of God, also called the Terrestrial Paradise, is the biblical paradise described in Genesis 2–3 and Ezekiel 28 and 31.

[14]Quote most often misattributed to the eighteenth-century Irish Philosopher and statesmen Edmund Burke, probably because President J. F. Kennedy did so in a speech before Canadian lawmakers in Ottawa, on May 17, 1961. Burke did say something resembling the quote in his "Thoughts on the Cause of the Present Discontents" (1770): "When bad men combine, the good must associate; else they will fall, one by one, an unpitied sacrifice in a contemptible struggle." Closer to the actual quote is what 1867 British philosopher John Stuart Mill said in his inaugural address to the University of St Andrews, "Bad men need nothing more to compass their ends, than that good men should look on and do nothing." See Reuters Fact Check Aug 9, 2020 at: https://www.reuters.com/article/factcheck-edmund-burke-quote/fact-check-edmund-burke-did-not-say-evil-triumphs-when-good-men-do-nothing-idUSL1N2PG1EY

[15]Walt Kelly, 1953 Pogo Comic Strip; Kelly coined the phrase during Senator Joe McCarthy's misguided hunt for alleged Communists in America causing widespread paranoia and turning neighbor against neighbor in a campaign of fear and hate. Kelly was saying that evil could be seen easily enough by gazing into the mirror.

[16]Mother Angelica, *Mother Angelica Live*, Talk Show, (EWTN, 1983-2001)

[17]Joyce Meyer, an American charismatic Christian author, speaker, and president of *Joyce Meyer Ministries*, (Instagram, Jan 7, 2019), Available at: https://www.instagram.com/p/BsWuTxmjS_y
The last line of the video is loosely quoted from John 16:33 where Jesus says, "In the world you face persecution. But take courage; I have conquered the world!"

[18]George MacDonald, *The Complete Works of George MacDonald*, (Kindle, Musaicum Books, 2017), MacDonald (1824-1905) was a Scottish author, poet, and Christian minister. He was a pioneering figure in the field of fantasy literature and the mentor of fellow writer Lewis Carroll.

[19]Jurgen Moltmann, *Theology of Hope: On the Ground and the Implications of a Christian Eschatology*, (New York: Harper & Row, 1967), Available at: http://media.sabda.org/alkitab-2/Religion-Online.org%20Books/Moltman%2C%20Jurgen%20-%20Theology%20of%20Hope.pdf

[20]Jurgen Moltmann, Available at: https://quotepark.com/quotes/1251582-jurgen-moltmann-god-weeps-with-us-so-that-we-may-one-day-laugh-wit/

[21]C. S. Lewis, *The Problem of Pain*, (New York: Macmillan, 1962)

[22]St. Augustine, *The City of God,* (Edinburg: T. & T. Clark, 1871), 1st Pub in Latin AD 426, Available at: https://books.google.com

[23]C. S. Lewis, *The Problem of Pain*, (New York: Macmillan, 1962), P. 197

[24]C. S. Lewis, *Mere Christianity*, (New York: Harper Collins, 1952)

[25]Pascal's Wager, from his *Pensées* [thoughts], (1669)

[26]"Acrisius". Play by Sophocles, Fragment 59

[27]https://mycatholicprayers.com/quotes/our-greatest-cross-is-the-fear-of-crosses/Our greatest cross is the fear of crosses. – My Catholic Prayers

[28]https://www.thecatholicthing.org/2015/01/11/john-vianney-and-the-cross/

[29]Mother Angelica, *Mother Angelica's Little Book of Life Lessons and Everyday Spirituality,* Ed. Raymond Arroyo, (New York: Doubleday, 2007), Also available at: https://www.azquotes.com/quote/462871

[30]Jurgen Moltmann, *Theology of Hope: On the Ground and the Implications of a Christian Eschatology,* (New York: Harper & Row, 1967)

[31]James Baldwin, in an essay for The New York Times published January 14, 1962; *The New York Times,* Section: The New York Times Book Review, "As Much Truth As One Can Bear," by James Baldwin, Start Page BR1, Quote Page BR38, Column 5, New York. (ProQuest)

[32]The author learned this phrase from friends who are active in Alcoholics Anonymous. It is a loose paraphrasing of many verses in the Bible. My favorites are Eph 3:20, 1 Peter 5:7, and, Exodus 14:14, "The Lord will fight for you, and you have only to keep still."

[33]Thomas Aquinas, *The Summa Theologica,* III, q. 49, ans. 3.

[34]Pope John Paul II, Apostolic Letter, *SALVIFICI DOLORIS,* Of The Supreme Pontiff, John Paul II On The Christian Meaning of Human Suffering; Given at Saint Peter's, Rome, on the liturgical Memorial of Our Lady of Lourdes, 11 February 1984, Libreria Editrice Vaticana, Available at: https://www.vatican.va/content/john-paul-ii/en/apost_letters/1984/documents/hf_jp-ii_apl_11021984_salvifici-doloris.html

[35]In 1991, prominent motivational author Anthony Robbins employed the saying, and he credited Dyer saying: "Recently, my feelings were put into words when I had the opportunity to visit with author Wayne Dyer. He said something that day that typifies my feelings. He told me, "We are not human beings having a spiritual experience. We are spiritual beings having a human experience." This quote is also attributed to Jesuit Priest Pierre Teilhard de Chardin (1881 – 1955), but it has not been referenced specifically to any of his writings.

[36]Eben Alexander, *Proof of Heaven,* (New York: Simon & Schuster, Oct. 23, 2012), ISBN: 1451695195, and "The Near-Death Experience of Deborah King", Anthony Chene Production, Nov 16, 2022, Available at: https://www.youtube.com/watch?v=eH3-WZWEMqY

[37]Lommel, Pim van, Ruud van Wees, Vincent Meyers, and Ingrid Elfferich. "Near-Death Experience in Survivors of Cardiac Arrest: A Prospective Study in the Netherlands." *The Lancet* 358, no. 9298 (December 15, 2001): 2039–2045.

[38]Parnia, S; Waller, DG; Yeates, R; Fenwick, P (2001). "A qualitative and quantitative study of the incidence, features and etiology of near-death experiences in cardiac arrest survivors". Resuscitation. 48 (2): 149–56. Also numerous other Parnia peer reviewed articles.

[39]Greyson B (2007). "Near-death experience: Clinical implications" (PDF). *Rev Psiq Clin*. 34: 116–125. See Bruce Greyson Wikipedia for many other books, articles, etc. Many available in PDf.

[40]Pascal's Wager, from his *Pensées*, (1669), as cited earlier

[41]Veritas Forum Talk, Harvard Medical School, Dec 19, 2014

[42]Karl A. Pillemer, Ph.D., Professor of Human Development, Cornell University; Author, "30 Lessons for Loving: Advice from the Wisest Americans on Love, Relationships, and Marriage"
Oct 16, 2013, 09:09 AM EDT; This post was published on the now-closed HuffPost Contributor platform. Contributors control their own work and posted freely to our site. Available at: https://www.huffpost.com/entry/fear-of-death_b_4075769

[43]Jeff Nixa, From his Oct. 28 2011 essay on Thomas Merton, Available at: https://urban-shamanism.org/tag/thomas-merton/

[44]Mother Angelica, as seen by the author in a *Mother Angelica Live* (1983-2001) rerun, March 28, 2023, Mother Angelica was best known as the founder of the international broadcast cable television network Eternal Word Television Network (EWTN).

Made in the USA
Monee, IL
17 October 2023

44749650R00059